The Power of BE!

An Initiation
Into the
Mysteries of
Soul Growth

Toni G. Boehm, Ph.D.

Inner Visioning Press
430 Winnebago Dr.
Greenwood, MO. 64034
816-537-5254 (F)
816-304-3044 ©

Published by Inner Visioning Press
Printed in the United States of America

The publisher wishes to thank and acknowledge
the design work of Gail Ishmael.

Library of Congress Control Number: 2010907358

The Power of BE!/Toni G. Boehm, Ph.D.

NEW ISBN # 978-0-9701537-6-0

1. Body, Mind and Spirit   2. Self-help
I.   Title The Power of BE!

Table of Contents

Dedication

This book is dedicated to my beloved uncle,
John D. Smittle.
Judge, your presence on this planet is missed!

Acknowledgments

There are always family members to acknowledge for their support and loyalty while one is writing and living amongst them, so rather, than make a list, just know that I love all of you.

To all of the authors who so graciously permitted the sharing of their work through this venue, thank you, thank you, thank you!

To Jay Boehm for his loving support – as always.

To the irreplaceable Gail Ishmael and her graphic support.

To the young people in our family: Courtlyn, Connor, Alexis, Lindsey, Lauren, Joshua, Demi, Sophia, Zander, Morgan, Mitchell, Carly, Jamie, and Eva Janelle – you have only just begun. You can do anything you focus your heart and intention on – Yes, You Can! I believe in you!

Chapter 1
Life at its Core is a Mystery

"Spiritual growth depends on concentrating
not on becoming but on, BE-ing."
--Eric Butterworth
Concentric Perspectives

"To discover the power of BE!
One must BE willing to sit at the edge of mystery.
At the edge of mystery as we sit in the silence and
actively contemplate life's mysteries, we are consciously
inviting the next "right" movement to arise.
For the edge of mystery is the place where the 'stirrings'
of the next "right" step begin to bubble;
where questions arise and answers ripen.
The edge of mystery is where quantum transformations
wait under the cover of darkness."
-Toni G. Boehm

Dancing at the Edge of Mystery

"I have come to teach you about what is,
and what was, and what will be
in order for you to understand the invisible world,
and the world that is visible,
and the immovable race of perfect humanity."[1]
--The Secret Book of John
The Nag Hammadi Library

Do you recall the scene in the *Indiana Jones* movie where the hero finds himself at what appears to be the edge of an abyss, an end-point with nowhere to go? Interestingly, in what appears to be an end-point is in fact a choice-point. For the hero pauses for a brief second, and contemplates the next step; which creates and forms his next action. Choice-point – will he choose to stay and face what he knows to be a certain fate or will he risk taking a step into the mystery of the unknown?

At this edge of mystery, he chooses and steps off into the unknown. Suddenly, out of seemingly nowhere, a platform rises up to support his foot and with every other step he takes, another platform appears and continues to support his steps until he reaches the other side.

At the edge of mystery, the hero makes a conscious choice; a choice that is made from a field of positive energy, of a willingness to reach farther, to

---

[1] Robinson, James. Nag Hammadi Library. Secret Book of John. Chapter 1.

move forward, and to release status quo – his choice is not made from fear, but from a desire for forward movement and action.

The edge of mystery is the place where we have the opportunity to extend our creative boundaries through acts of positive and conscious choices. We call them conscious choices because we must consciously say "yes" to forward movement, "yes" to the next risk, "yes" to the releasing of status quo, and "yes" to the next authentic step.

Choice-point moments offer us the option to stay and do what we have always done – for this is relatively safe and without much jeopardy on our part. Alternatively, they offer us the opportunity to be a part of the unfoldment of a new possibility; however, to do this we often have to take a risk. We must risk the taking of a step into the unknown and finding out what it is that "possibility" has waiting for us as we extend the boundaries of our current state of awareness.

The edge of mystery is the place where the "stirrings" of new growth and next steps begin to bubble, where we allow questions to take form and answers to ripen; and new questions to arise from what we thought were *the* answers.

Through this act of giving questions conscious permission to continually rise and re-form, we find that we do not focus as much on discovering accurate, right and/or correct answers to our questions, as we do on allowing the next question to form, rise, and come into conscious awareness. It is the questions and not their answers, per se`, which lead us into new shifts in awareness.

The edge of mystery is the periphery or rim of the starting point for the next movement of growth and its experiences. Whether we realize it or not, the call for this new growth and movement does not arise from outside sources, although it may appear that way. It may appear that someone or something is forcing us or asking us to change, move, release, let go, and so forth; but, in actuality, the call to dance at the edge of mystery comes from within. It ascends from a place that resides deep in the interior spaces of our soul, from the unified-energetic field that we are connected to and that we are made of and from.

Why do we say this call for movement, growth, and expansion arises from a soul or unified field level? Because when we are "ripe", as in seasoned, ready and/or mature, for growth in conscious awareness; when we are ready for expansion of thought and ensuing action, and/or when we desire to experience something new, "the field energy that surrounds us" and our soul, calls us into a right and perfect experience. An experience that will call forth the next phase of growth and/or maturity.

Our agreement to participate in the growth or not – for we can always choose to remain in status quo – determines the amount of happiness or pain we continue to experience.

*"Do what you have always done and
you will get more of what you already got!"*

Dancing at the Edge of Mystery: What Does That Mean???

Dancing at the edge of mystery (D.E.M.) is a metaphor for those moments when our soul, in cooperation with the infinite invisible universal energy field, invites us to move deeper into an experience that will unveil another layer of the essence and power of who we truly are – who we truly *BE*!

When we are willing to dance at the edge of mystery we are invited by the unseen universal forces to:

*Extend, erase, or dissolve the illusion of boundaries and limitations which we have created in our minds and then ultimately, express and experience in our lives. To know that we have placed these boundaries and limitations upon ourselves – even if they appear to come from outside ourselves. To know that through "right" timing and synchro-divinity we are now, consciously or unconsciously, ready to expand our boundaries, and release imposed limitations in order to move deeper into the conscious awareness of *BE*!

*Create conscious choices which have the potential to move us into processes of conscious change and quantum transformation. Conscious choice, combined with concentrated attention and clarity of intention, has the potential to be life altering.

BE in the midst of mystery of questions arising around us, and to *BE* comfortable not knowing the answers. To allow the "death-maturation" process of the ego-self to continually emerge, so that who we *BE* may be revealed.

BE interested in the energy arising around us in the moment and what it desires to reveal and *BE* interested in the choices we are called to consider and how they add to the possibility of growth and/or a shift in consciousness, or not.

BE interested in the mystery of synchro-divinity (synchronicity) and intuition as forms of guidance for our lives. To be open and receptive to the movement of spiritual energies known as intuition; and to feel its "hits" and "nudges" calling us into its deeper mystery.

*Discern how to "consciously live" in *"BE" awareness. BE* is an active state of being in tune and one with the principles, ideas, and + energies that arise around us. e.g., I consciously *BE* Peace. I *BE* Love. I *BE* Authentic.   I no longer seek these things, I *BE* them.

*Pray, meditate, contemplate, practice self-observation and self-honesty; when we do this we begin to see the adverse ego-self and it shadows in relation to the True _Self. These revelations have the capacity to call forth spiritual en'lighten'ment, quantum leaps in awareness and transformation, and 21st century creative partnerships.

The Quantum (-Q-) Field Mystery

As was stated, when we dance at the edge of mystery, our greatest potential lies in the asking of the questions, and not necessarily in the discovery of the answers. Through the simple acts of *ask and inquiry* possibility arises, possibility that can lead us into new shifts in awareness.

A simple question such as, "What do I want to be when I grow up?" – asked by a teen or an adult – has the potential to initiate a "shift" in conscious awareness that can have a great impact on the rest of one's life.

How does this "shift", movement, or leap in awareness occur? It happens when there is a alignment of the "energies" held within the invisible, unified-energy field that we live and move within. In this moment of energetic-alignment, "shift" happens. The "shift" occurs first in consciousness and then becomes visible as an effect that is seen in the world.

It is this infinite field of possibility and potential that has the capacity to awaken us to who we truly BE! This *field of infinite potential* is referred to in this book with the use of the symbol -Q-. -Q- is defined in the following ways:

-Q- : the invisible, infinite, universal, energetic, quantum-unified field that underlies everything.

–Q-: the energetic-field that we imprint our thought-intentions upon and thus, create our world out of.

-Q-: refers to a momentary energetic alignment within our energy field of all the elements necessary for a new idea or awareness to come into mind, as an "ah-ha." When a -Q- an energetic "shift" is initiated, that moment has the potential to move us into a edge of mystery where the next awakening experience resides.

Can we support the universe in the creation of energetically aligned –Q- moments? YES! How? Through being a transparency, without hidden agendas or motives. Transparency opens *for* more Light, Illumination, and Divine Ideas to move through us! So, how do we *BE* transparent?

We gain transparency, as we willingly let go of the secrets, lies, and negative emotions we have been hiding behind. When we are willing to honestly, begin to observe our behaviors and actions and when we realize that the secrets and lies we hiding behind and hiding from are not only toxic to our being but they hide our true essence. They are toxic to our body for they create *energetic sludge* that lives in the deep recesses of our mind. This "sludge" blocks the *Light* of potential and possibility. It is the light of understanding that is the way to gain true freedom and happiness.

Thus, the more transparent we are willing to *BE*, the more energetic-thought sludge or baggage we are willing to release, the more *Light* or understanding of what is true and real can be revealed in mind and shine through our consciousness.

Transparency also comes about by being willing to *BE* conscious. We become conscious, as we engage in forgiveness, prayer, affirmations and denials, meditation, "shadow" cleanup work, self-observation, and by saying "yes" to the taking of authentic actions. Just to name a few of the ways.

Alignment with the Q-field is not some great difficult process; it can come about in "a twinkling of an eye. Each time an alignment occurs we *BE* a little more transparent and the more transparent we are the more *Light* is emitted. This movement of energy is circular and spirals up; it is a never-ending, upward movement of growth.

Authors, Gary Simmons and Rima Bonario in their book, *The Art and Practice of Living with Nothing and No One Against Me,* speak of the -Q-Effect[2] and -Q- Territory. Other authors are expressing ideas such as, The -Q-Project, -Q- Marketing Solutions, -Q- Therapy, and the list goes on. In this book, we use -Q- edge, -Q- momentum, -Q- creation, -Q- transformation, -Q- organizations, -Q- leadership... We can see that -Q- awareness is revealing itself in consciousness in a multitude of ways, dimensions, and definitions.

The -Q- field's capacity to affect and create shift is because there is an interconnectedness of all things – this is scientifically being proven. The affect once it occurs, changes not only the individual, but it also affects the consciousness of what is called, the collective. Additionally, both the individual and the collective awareness's are affected or changed both on an

[2] Simmons, Gary and Bonario, Rima. *The Art and Practice of Living with Nothing and No One Against Me. The Q Effect Publications. Lees Summit, MO.*

interior and exterior level, as well. Meaning that something happens, the shift occurs, in mind and in manifestation, the outer.

Interiorly, the effect happens as a shift or change in conscious awareness. Exteriorly, the shift expresses as a manifestation of change in our life conditions, values, and/or circumstances. What affects the individual, ultimately affects the collective whole of humanity; as we are all inter-connected at the quantum level. This inter-engagement and full impact scenario is what Ken Wilber refers to as the Integral Vision[3] or AQAL. All Quadrants, All Levels.

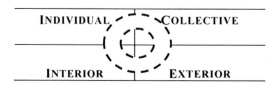

It is important to remember that as AQAL occurs, chaos may ensue. Being integral and aligning with a new field of awareness does not ensure peace, and that all is well. Change, shift, and transformation require a movement on all levels of being; and the disruption may not be pretty.

e.g., A simplistic example. A woman (*an individual*) victimized (*in mind and body – interior and exterior*) by her spouse and finally says, *no more;* and goes to a therapist. Through therapy and connecting with who she is interiorly, the woman begins to shift into new levels of awareness and her confidence builds (*interior change in mind occurs*). This shift in awareness leads her to seek a change in her life-style (*exterior result of interior shift in awareness*), and a divorce ensues (*collective impacted by interior change*). The woman's internal shift in awareness created an external effect and the change in her as an individual, affected the collective whole of the family. AQAL was experienced through a shift in awareness occurring and that shift created a change in the outer. All four quadrants were involved in the change.

Throughout this book, the word integral is referred to. Integral is that which is vital, primary, embracing, balancing, inclusive, essential, and central. When referred to in the context of human beings integral means, "*models, maps, and practices that include the full spectrum of human potentials*".

We develop an integral perspective physical, mentally, emotionally, and spiritually as we successfully integrate the various states and stages of development, such as Abraham Maslow's *Hierarchy of Needs* or Carl Jung's *Four Archetypes*. Integration of the developmental states and/or stages of life affect how we see and perceive life

---

[3] Wilber, Ken. *A Theory of Everything*. Shambala. Boston, MA. 2001.

*"Life is an upward, progressive, ever-evolving
spiral of expanding consciousness."*
--Silent Unity Affirmation
(early years)

Another View of the -Q- Edge Chart

This chart is a symbolic representation of how a movement or interaction
has the capacity to lead us to an awakening, a shift in awareness, or a new
state or stage of development; all based upon our choices. The gateway
for entering into life's balance and wisdom is through consciously
integrating all of the quadrants.

Individual
1st we are *Unconscious*
then we become *Self-Aware*
through *Self-Observation* which
leads to doing
Shadow-Work which leads to
Self-Transcendence→*BE*

Collective
1st there is a state of
Status Quo then a *Change*
or *Catalyst* arises and often
Chaos ensues to force the
change: result, a
Paradigm Shift occurs

Internal
1st we are Asleep
Then we Awake which creates a
Shift or Quantum Leap in Mind
Which Calls Forth a
Transformation

External
1st we are *Complacent* then
a *New Choice, Value, or
Information* comes into
Awareness that *Forces
Change and New Choice or
Value* is *Established*

*"Evolution is the emergence
of that which already is
...the whole process of evolution
is to produce a being who can consciously co-operate
with the Evolutionary Principle, which is Pure Spirit."*
--Ernest Holmes

Conscious Choice-Point Moments

Regardless, of what circumstances bring us to dance at the edge of
mystery, the edge is where the possibility for change exists. The edge holds
the potential for quantum leaps in mind that can lead to deep transformative
experiences. The edge is a choice-point; the edge is a still-point; and the edge

holds the potential and possibility for soul growth within its grasp at all times, depending upon the choices we make. Soul growth is entirely dependent upon, whether we choose to be conscious or unconscious in our decision-making and subsequent actions.

We define consciousness as awareness, being reflective, aware of, and self-observant to that which is occurring around and within us. Consciousness provides us with the ability to be self-reflective and to be conscious and aware of our thoughts, behaviors, and beliefs and how they influence our life experiences. We create our life experiences through the perceptions we hold in consciousness, our conscious and subconscious minds. Our perceptions are a result of our thoughts and feelings about what has happened to us as a result of our life experiences. Our perceptions are the meaning we give to our life experiences. Life has only the meaning we give it – ponder this statement – it has the capacity to influence the rest of your life!

We are conscious when we are aware of what is happening energetically in, around, and through us in any given moment. If we arrive at an edge moment and choose to stay unconscious; fighting, lying, cheating, denying, addicted, numb, projecting, and so on – so that we can appear to be right, in control, looking good, in charge, cool, slick, happy, not hurting, not caring, etc. – our transformation will be minimal, if at all.

To dance at the edge of mystery invites us to make conscious choices, to participate in awakening, self-observation, self-questioning, self-reflection, deep contemplation and meditation, and ultimately the taking of authentic actions. It is the point where seeking stops and learning to *BE* is initiated; we stop seeking and *BE* the principles we say we believe in, in action.

Often, we awaken – or become conscious of the impact of our thoughts, behaviors and actions – because a moment of clarity reveals to us a new possibility for interacting with life's experiences, our perceptions about something, and or our life conditions. An awakening is an "ah-ha" moment, which says, "yes" I understand! I do not have to do life this way again – I have the power to make new choices!

*"The degree to which you are willing and able
to quickly shift the focus of your attention when called for,
is the degree to which you are awake in that moment."*

The edge of mystery is the place where the -Q- energy field moves and impels us through an invisible desire to grow beyond our current thought-limitations and beliefs. Being at the edge often necessitates a movement into an area that is unfamiliar and requires us to take new and authentic actions. To *BE* authentic means that we are genuine in the expression of our thoughts, feelings, behaviors, and actions and in the expression of those we hurt no one else.

e.g., in any moment, we can make the choice to lie to someone or to tell the truth. Choice-point moments occur when we decide which behavior or thought we will choose to engage. When we recognize that we have choices, (one of which is not to lie) and we consciously stop and weigh how our choices will serve us and/or others, and we make the decision *not* to lie – we are engaging authentic-self action.

Taking Authentic Actions

Authentic-self action (internal focused) and authentic action (external focused) is a result of a combination of conscious awareness, self-observation, self-honesty, and conscious choice/s. All of which combine and allow for an outcome that holds for the highest and best for all persons involved.

Authentic actions require a level of surrender and trust because most of time we would rather not take authentic actions, for they require too much of us. We would rather live with status quo or take the easy way out – but the "Universe Impulse" in alignment with our soul will not let us do that. That is why we call them authentic actions.

Authentic actions move us into responses that call for – truth, transparency, vulnerability, self-honesty, self-nakedness, and authenticity – all of which contain the possible for the exposure of who we are, with all our foibles. What we find when we choose to risk the exposure of the little "i" or little ego-self is that people already have seen our flaws and foibles and decided they would like us anyway. And we thought we were doing such a great job of hiding our "stuff"!

When we are conscious, we stop and take notice. We stop, as in, take a breath, and look around us and notice what is really going on; and we become interested in what we are noticing.

For instance, we stop, take notice, and become interested in, why we think that a choice to lie would be better than telling the truth. Because we are noticing, we now have the capacity to reflect honestly on what we would gain by lying.

Are we lying in order that we might be thought of as looking good, capable, appearing as perfect, able to get things done, a mover and shaker ...

When we are conscious we have the capacity to look honestly at what is happening around and within us, and we are interested in what we are seeing. When we are interested in what we are seeing, we are then willing to tell the truth about what we are seeing. This is big, for in order to grow we must notice and be interested in what has the potential to create growth.

When we are conscious of what or how we are thinking, feeling, saying, and acting we have the opportunity to gain insight and clarity into the motives and fears behind them and the choices they lead us into making. These insights, however small, have the capacity to initiate an honest internal self-dialogue. Honest self-dialogue invites us to make new choices; choices that often result in, participation in actions that are more authentic actions.

It doesn't matter if the choices before us are about – getting married, taking a new job, leaving the security of an old job, getting a divorce, having a baby, letting our children grow up and leave home, or growing spiritually. It all comes down to whether we will choose to make a conscious decision for our life or whether "life" will make the decision for us.

When we choose to make conscious decisions it often leads us to the edge of what we currently know and invites us to take a step out of that current knowing into the mystery of the unknown. This is how we extend the boundaries of our current awareness and life experiences.

At times, choice-point moments of conscious decision-making call for actions that require instantaneous pronouncements; and at other times, it requires going to the edge to sit and be in the mystery as we patiently wait for our next steps to be revealed. The question is "Does the edge of mystery interest you or scare you?"

> *"Our freedom extends only as far as our*
> *consciousness reaches.*
> *Beyond that we succumb to the unconscious influences*
> *of our environment"*[4]
> — Carl Jung

A Conscious Surrender into the Mystery

> *"Those who seek should not stop seeking until they find.*
> *When they find, they will be disturbed.*
> *When they are disturbed, they will marvel,*
> *and will reign over all.*
> *And after they have reigned they will rest.]".*[5]
> --Gospel of Thomas;
> *The Nag Hammadi Library*

Quantum physics research is confirming through empirical data that humankind, both individually and as a collective whole, is a creative partner in the act of creation. Through our mind – our thoughts and feelings – intentions, choices of where to place our attention, and perceptions – we work in cooperation with a quantum field of energy to create results or not.

In new thought spirituality or metaphysics this is called, working with the law. Law is a rule of action and law is impartial, the law works in accordance with how you work it – it is your choice as to whether you will work with it a

---

[4] Jung, Carl. *Collected Works 13, Alchemical Studies*. Princeton/Bollinger. New York. pg. 118

[5] Patterson, Stephen and Meyer, Marvin (Trans.). *The Nag Hammadi Library*. Gnostic Society. Logion 2

positive way or a negative way. The Law works (begins forth results) in accordance with how you choose to work it! The law works as you work it!

Scientific research is now verifying what teachers of new thought spirituality have taught for centuries – that *thoughts held in mind produce in the outer after their kind.* We are conscious creative partners and our efforts are rewarded through "laboring" in resonant fields of energy; fields which return to us that which we have seeded and tended within them. As conscious 21st century creative beings we have the capacity to imprint our intentions upon the fabric of the universal energy and generate a better world for all sentient beings and ourselves.

As stated, quantum physics, along with medicine, psychology, pharmacology, engineering, and other modalities are now empirically providing data which reveals what teachers of spirituality have been teaching for years – that each of us has the energetic potential within us to generate ideas that can ultimately benefit the good of all and at the same time evolve the consciousness of humanity.

Humankind, as a whole, evolves through the creation of new collective value-sets or memes, that we accept as true; e.g., Modern medicine has researched and discovered cures for diseases, such as scurvy (a lack of vitamin C), that killed thousands of people at one time. Pharmacology has developed medicines and vaccines that support the longevity of humankind. Through engineering marvels, we have designed space ships that take us to the moon and telescopes that allow us to see into black holes, space, and its universes beyond. Psychology has opened doorways into the mind, through proper counseling and other modalities of support, that allows for persons with mental issues to maintain a life that works.

Quantum physics is revealing that at the sub-atomic or quanta level, everything is interrelated and interconnected. Quantum researchers are validating that the fabric of reality is permeated with a substance that causes it to expand in response to a collection of thoughts, feelings, and observation.

Friends, we are dancing at the edge of mystery. Revelations are being made that might even boggle the minds of those great spiritual teachers who preceded us, such as Buddha, Jesus Christ, Lao-Tze, Confucius, Moses, Isaiah, Mohammed, and many others who paved the way for the concepts of this day and age to be revealed and ultimately accepted.

We have made a turn on the spiral of evolution and ours is a different time and space; there are new discoveries to made, within and without. As a collective whole, humanity is invited to step into the mystery of what desires to be revealed in this specific age of spiritual growth and awareness.

Synchronicity and Synchro-Divinity

"Space, time, physical and temporal boundaries,
culture, religion, and ethnic heritage are illusions,
created by mind to keep us in a sense of separation.
Once recognized – the great Truth – we are all One,
our intuition calls to act in bolder and greater ways.
Synchronistic encounters are meaningful
and are manifestations of an invisible power working."
--Carl Jung

"Synchronicities are people, places, or events that your soul attracts
into your life – to help you evolve or to place emphasis on something going
on in your life. The more 'consciously aware' you become of how your
soul creates – the higher your frequency goes
and the faster your soul manifests.
Each day your life will become filled with meaningful coincidences -
synchronicities - that you have attracted – or created in the grid of your
experiences in the physical."
--Author Unknown

When an experiment or discovery in quantum physics is discussed, be assured that whatever theory or hypothesis the scientist is currently working on, their study is only considered valid when their phenomena is reproducible and quantifiable. Synchronicity, however, is not one of those scientifically provable theories – yet!

Synchronistic events (*"synchro-divinities"*) are said to come to us because we are energetically at the right place at the right time, we are ready for the lesson or idea that is ripe to be emphasized, and/or other reasons yet not known that we are prepared for in consciousness.

Just because synchronistic events are not quantifiable, does not mean, that they are not valid or are not real. Some things in this world are and always will remain indefinable, non-quantifiable, and non-reproducible scientifically.

Synchronicities come into play – all the time – and they are not just about thinking of someone and they appear. As we open our consciousness to the idea that there is this indefinable process and experience, synchronicities start to become woven into the fabric of our every day existence. There are appointed times for everything. The information of when it is the "right" time to do something enters the -Q- or quantum resonant unified field of energy around us and moves into our conscious awareness appearing as a type of synchronistic event.

When a synchronistic event occurs, often it is accompanied by a choice-point moment; a time that calls for an action or forward movement. In this choice-point moment, we decide if we will align with the action or not – consciously choosing to participate or not. This action or decision can be as simple as choosing to read the book that has fallen off the table, at our feet, or not. If we say "yes!" to whatever the action is, usually our lives are impacted in some form from it or, it triggers another experience to unfold.

The more aligned we are with the -Q- field that surrounds us, the more this energy removes obstacles and creates openings for change and growth. Energy is a living substance that surrounds us and we create form through and with it. Learn to cooperate with the -Q- field and it will bring to you what you need and will do it through synchronistic events. Be on the look out!

Intuition – Our Inner Guidance System

Intuition arises from a place of "mystery", from tapping into the –Q- field of knowledge that resides within and around us. Just like synchro-divinity, intuition's mysterious messages may not be able to explained or rationalized from a mental perspective. But "know" that the guidance given is real and it usually demands something from us. The guidance we receive challenges us to trust, to consciously be willing to lay aside pre-conceived notions and reliance on facts, to move forward in faith, etc.

We may go to others for advice, but even then, it is up to us, to make the decision to follow their suggestions or not. We must turn to our own wisdom for the ultimate determination. Our internal intuitive system is forever trying to make itself known to us, but we tend to shut it out because we do not trust it to lead us in the right direction.

Even though we all have the intuitive capability, very few refer to it as a tool for everyday living. We tend to be skeptical of this faculty and would rather rely on something more tangible – cold, hard facts.

Why is it that we do not inherently trust this intuitive response system? Could it be perhaps because, over the centuries, intuition has been labeled as an emotionally based "woman-thing"; a feminine-oriented trait? Thus, it has not been considered as an acceptable, reliable, or credible as a form of information gathering.

From an intellectual (masculine-oriented) perspective, it is only after we have gathered all the rational facts and empirical data that we can then determine what to do next. This is not about right or wrong, blame, etc.; it is just a report on probable cause.

Does this mean that if we regularly follow our "intuitive hits" that we would never rely on outer facts or observations? "NO." Everything in life is meant to be part of our decision-making process, but the final nudge--the yea or nay--is meant to come from within.

When one engages in this intuitive approach as a way of living life it becomes an internal cycle of response. We receive a "spiritual hit", we trust it's message, we take action on the guidance given, and the process starts all over again. After a while, more and more intuitive messages seem to come, until finally every aspect of our life is turned over to this internal intuitive guidance system.

Like Jacob, with his vision of the angels and the ladder we must create the space, energetically, for intuitive hits to arise; we do this through being open and sensitive to the idea and to the possibility that a greater mystery is working in us and desires to teach us more about who we are.

Intuition is often defined as the ability to know the future, but this is not truly, what it means. Prophecy is the word that better defines the ability to make future projections.

Intuition is about the energy of what is happening in the moment and being alert to the energetic "messages" that desire to be recognized. These messages can affect your future, but do not necessarily reveal it. Intuition is guidance for the moment.

Charles Fillmore, a new thought writer of the early 20th century and co-founder of Unity School of Christianity, states in his book, *The Revealing Word* (pg. 108) that intuition is:

"The natural knowing capacity. Inner knowing; the immediate apprehension of ... Truth without resort to intellectual means. The wisdom of the heart. It is very much surer in guidance than the head...Through the power of intuition, [humankind] has direct access to all knowledge..."

According to modern day author, Caroline Myss, in her book "*Why People Don't Heal And How They Can.*" the root of our intuitive ability comes from having a strong sense of self-esteem. If we think about this concept, it makes sense.

When a person has low self-esteem they are more vulnerable to the opinions of others and are usually in a constant quandary as to what to do next. People with low self-esteem tend to doubt that their opinion count – so why would they believe something as intangible as an intuitive hit.

It takes a sense of courage and knowing who one is to follow through on the intuitive hits, guidance, nudges, and ideas received.

> *"As a farmer removes the dirt from a ditch*
> *so water may flow to nourish his crops, so too must we*
> *remove the obstacles from our mind in order*
> *for Spirit's energy to freely flow.'*
> --Pantajali: a paraphrase

In the Energetic Flow of Life: a Personal Reflection

When an "urge" of a project forming is felt, I wait until an intuitive nudge is received that "says", it is time to begin. Until then, I sit in the question and dance at the edge of mystery with the ideas, giving them to germinate and take root.

Sometimes this act of waiting takes only a few hours, and at other times, it takes days or weeks. In this "waiting" time, "right" alignment with the –Q- field is being created.

This act of waiting – with expectancy – is not the same as procrastination. The energetic resonant field that we live in has antennas, it "knows" what thought-energies are being imprinted upon it and it returns to us the same resonant-type energy.

What this means is that if we procrastinate, which is not pure or pristine energy, the field will reflect that same type of defer-delay energy back to us, in our work and life.

Waiting with a sense of expectancy, doing what we need to do in the moment, and yet knowing that the right and perfect – book, person, or addition to the project is aligning with us through the –Q- field – opens the way for more of the same possibility-type energy to be returned to us.

Additionally, when we wait with a sense of spaciousness, we create an energetic opening in consciousness, which allows for completion of our work or project, with less energy than if we would have forced a movement. Energy does not lie and it cannot be fooled with.

The intuitive nudge that informs us that it is time to proceed, to take authentic action – is action rooted in guidance and assurance that arises from a higher Source than the personal ego-self.

As we dance at the edge of mystery; in the momentum of the -Q- field – the universal energetic flow of life – we do not necessarily know where the energy will take us, but we can rest assured that we are being led!

The Seed of Mystery is Planted

> *"Know what is in front of your face,*
> *and what is hidden from you will be disclosed to you.*
> *For there is nothing hidden that will not be revealed.*
> *[And there is nothing buried that will not be raised.]"*[6]
> --Gospel of Thomas;
> *The Nag Hammadi Library*

At the age of 28 years I began my conscious pursuit of this mystery called spiritual en'lighten'ment; and now, I can say, with all my heart, that *it* actually pursued me. Until then, God, Spirit, Higher Power, and the spiritual path had been lost to me, or at the very least, put behind me.

---

[6] Patterson, Stephen and Meyer, Marvin (Trans.). *The Nag Hammadi Library*. Gnostic Society. Logion 5

I was born and raised in Pennsylvania. My birth father was of Italian heritage and did not play a role in my life after the age of three, when he left to get a loaf of bread and never returned. My mother was mentally ill and thus, my life and that of my sisters, was always in a state of chaos. Stability was not necessarily a component of my mother's life repertoire and was similarly reflected in our day-to-day existence.

One of the things that my mom loved to do, however, was to go to church; she would move us from church to church. Every few months we would try a new church or attend weeklong revivals held by persons such as Kathryn Coleman or A.A. Allen. My first memory was of the Church of Christ where I was baptized by immersion. We then moved on to the Lutheran church where I received confirmation. Confirmation of what? Today I am still not sure. Finally, and perhaps the most impacting upon my child psyche, we attended the Pentecostal church.

I speak of the impact of the Pentecostal experience for two reasons. First, it fascinated me as to how this thing called the "Holy Spirit" could enter a body and create such an emotional upheaval in the name of revelation. Secondly, it was at a Pentecostal revival, at the age of eight or nine that I first heard about the Mayan calendar.

The minister was standing in the front of the lectern and we were in the front row. He had worked himself into a frenzy telling us about what horrid creatures we were. He was so close to me, that I could reach out and touch him and I could smell the sweat upon his body. It was at that moment when I was aware of his closeness, that he dropped the bomb!

He said that the Mayan calendar would end at the year 2012 and so would the world! I still remember his words to this day. The emotional assault I felt was overpowering and I was shocked and stunned. My little psyche had just been assailed, for not only was I not worth so much, as a worm of the earth; but in 2012 – if I lived that long – I was going to die anyway! The world was going to end. I remember thinking, "This cannot be so! I will find out the truth of all this!"

Perhaps that is the day my spiritual quest began. However, after a few weeks of my curious eight-year-old mind delving and questioning and finding no real answers to calm my harried soul; I decided to let it all go. I decided that I would just wait and see what would happen; perhaps the minister was wrong.

I look back over my life and I see this moment in time, as my first attempt at surrender; for I surrendered the question of the end of the world into the mystery of the unknown. I believe that night a seed was planted in my mind and that seed grew into a desire to understand – not what it means to live in end times – but what it means to "dance at the edge of mystery" and how to live with the questions that arise there.

Upon reflection of my life experiences, I have now reached a point in my spiritual development where I can say with all honesty that I bless my parents for all the experiences they provided me and the roles they assumed; for they ultimately shaped my spiritual destiny.

Stepping into the Mystery of the Little Blue Planet

> *"The lower self is not so much a thing as a process*
> *created by the interaction of the soul and the body.*
> *Body and soul are pure and blameless in themselves.*
> *However, when our soul becomes embodied,*
> *we tend to forget our soul-nature,*
> *we become attached to the world and*
> *develop such qualities as greed, lust, and pride."*[7]
> --The Essential Sufism

Permit me to share a tale with you. Over the years, I have heard several variations of this story, so in the name of integrity I will give credit to my latest source[8] and share a paraphrased version.

The tale is one of intrigue and possibility; of how it is that we might step into this mystery known as life and begin to dance at the edge of mystery. The first time I read this story, it created a vibration that resonated deep in my soul. As it is a tale of mystery and possibility, I invite you to be open to allowing its words to dance across the synapses of your mind and heart and to create images that give shape to the story and bring it to life for you.

Let possibility and potential collide and deeper questions arise for certainly there is no-way of knowing for sure if the story is real; but, "what if?"

The Embodiment Team: Do You Feel a Vibratory Resonance?

Imagine that you are living in paradise, wandering about without any cares, problems, or concerns. You are happy, contented, and free. However, you do not have a body! Your current assignment is paradise, located between the worlds. You are here in paradise awaiting your next mission. Interestingly, you can't remember if you have been in this state for a long time or, if it was just yesterday that you came here." It does not matter really, for you are happy being in the state you are.

Upon awakening one morning, a vibration touches you. It is a vibration emitted from the Embodiment Team – it comes only on occasion. The team is asking if anyone is ready to take form. They are looking for a few souls who have a vibratory resonance with the call and assignment sent forth at this

---

[7] Fadiman, James and Frager, Roger (eds). *The Essential Sufism.* pg.65.
[8] Simmons, Gary: *The I of the Storm*: Unity House. Unity Village, MO. 2001. pgs.1-3

time. Apparently, a small blue planet in the Milky Way Galaxy is in crisis and they need help.

You notice that the vibration interests you; you feel it deeply, and you resonate with the vibration. You step forth and say, "Yes! I am ready let me serve! Use me!"

However, prior to final selection, it is customary that you go before the Embodiment and Incarnation Team. Somewhere from within your soul you feel this is your assignment. You feel ready to go! You go before the Embodiment and Incarnation Team to dialogue about the resonate feelings you are experiencing. They are interested in knowing what you want to learn and what was it about this call that created a stirring within your energy strings.

They ask many questions and the more they ask, the more you are certain that it is time to go back into a body and that Earth is your assignment. Upon completing your session with the Team it is ascertained that, "Yes, indeed", a resonant field is there. The team requests that you create a "Covenant of Experience".

This Covenant of Experience frees you to take a body, to go forth to serve, and to grow spiritually while serving. It assures you a place in a family and the guarantee that you will experience situations and/or conditions that will create maximum growth for your soul.

Together with the E&I Team you co-create a custom-designed learning curriculum for *your* incarnation. A curriculum that is of maximum service to your soul's growth – after all, why waste an incarnation?

During your time with the team, you decide what gifts, talents, dreams, goals, family, birth date, astrological sign, race, ethnicity, gender, socio-economic class, religion, name, and identity you will take on. All of which are designed to facilitate and to support the highest and best for your soul's growth.

Oh, yes! In addition, you agree that when you get to the little blue planet, you will forget about the Team and the Covenant for a period of time. This time span depends upon how much you are willing to learn and to grow through the experiences that have been created for you.

You arrive on the blue planet and you do forget who you are and that you are in the midst of a maximum learning experience. You forget that you are there to help, grow, and be in service to humankind. You forget and you start to identify with the story. Indeed, you believe you are the story that you co-created with the Team.

You begin to give your new identity great meaning and you use it to look at everything you do; especially in the creation of your relationships. You become so mesmerized by this illusion that you forget the mystery of where you came from and who you really are – a soul on a journey with a purpose. That, my friend, is why the acts of universal synchronicity have brought you to this story. It is time for you to remember – time to *BE*! Are you ready?

NOTE: *A Mystery Practice is designed to assist and support you in the unfolding of the transparency in consciousness, in calling forth transformation and wholeness; creating a 21st century consciousness of BE!*

A "Mystery" Practice: A "Covenant of Experience"

This is a "what-if" experience, you are invited to "dance in the mystery" with possibility. For this experience, you will need a piece of paper and a pen. If you are in a group, when directed, find a partner, preferably someone you do not know very well.

For one (1) minute, in big picture-type ideas, list all the experiences, values, family situations, etc., that could have come from the creation of a personal, Covenant of Experience – if there were such a thing.

List those things that have affected, influenced, or impacted your life significantly – both positive and negative. If possible, start from the time prior to your birth.

If in a group, share the contents of your Covenant of Experience with a partner. (If alone, journal for one minute, using the same guidelines.) Do not hesitate or think about what you are to say, let it flow! Just go for it! Let it flow and see what desires to come forth from the depths of your being.

After the sharing (or writing, if alone) is complete, being very gentle with yourself, take a few moments to review your list and what you shared. What do you notice?

Be very honest with your observations, insights, and feelings; what came forth that you did not expect, if anything? This exercise is a way to begin the process of learning how to be conscious to what is energetically arising within us in the moment.

Does It Interest You – What Do You Notice?

> *"Keep knocking, and the joy inside*
> *will eventually open a window and*
> *look to see who's there."*
> --Rumi [9]

"Does it interest you?" and "What are you noticing?" These are what I refer to as 21st century consciousness raising questions. It was in the presence of a great coach, Maria Nemeth [10] that these questions came alive for me. Through her coaching expertise, I began to notice and to be interested in what I was noticing.

---

[9] Barks, Coleman. *The Poetry of Rumi Journal*. Brush Dance Publications. Sausalito, CA.

[10] Nemeth, Maria. *The Energy of Money*. Ballentine Wellspring. New York, N.Y. 1999. Academy for Coaching Excellence. Sacramento, CA.

I have since realized that although these two questions are small in nature (four words each) they are immense in potential. They have the capacity to stir soul growth and aid in the personal evolution of consciousness – if we allow them! These two questions are akin to the great question, "Who am I?"

For centuries, mystics have spoken of the power inherent in the question; "Who am I?" Why, because in order to ask the question one must be awake and searching, or at least ready to journey deeper into the mystery of self and Self.

"Does it interest you?" "What are you noticing?" These questions invite us to *BE* awake to the energy that surrounds and that always desires to share energetic information with us. The problem is we do not know how to listen and hear.

By noticing and being interested in what we are noticing, we *BE* conscious. By being conscious we are open to the possibility of participating in our experiences in a more cognizant manner and with a sense of grace and ease. We become more interested in the energy arising within the experience of the moment – than the drama the moment might be presenting. Being more interested in the energy arising, supports in shifting focus so we can release our attachment to outcomes, judgments, comparisons, and so much more.

Review the following questions and practice noticing and being interested in the energy they call forth from within your being. Do not let your mind take you on a journey to find an answer to the question, just dance with its mystery. Just be interested in what the questions stir within your soul for having been asked. Be willing to sit at the edge of mystery with each question, for a short period of time.

A "Mystery" Practice: Does This Interest Me?

Being with the Questions: Does This Interest Me?
What do I Notice About Being Interested?

Instructions:

Sit in the mystery of these questions and when the time is ripe – and you will know when that is – journal about what you notice. What arose as you sat with the questions?

Our work is to hone our awareness to the point that we *BE* conscious; aware and awake to the energies moving around and within us. From that space of awareness, we utilize these energies to co-create a higher wisdom and/or an expanded, more positive, response to our experiences.

We *BE* conscious as we *BE* more interested in what is arising energetically – as a lesson or learning – than in what appears to be happening as our current experience.

Does it interest me enough to ask myself: Who am I? Why do I exist? Who is God? What is God? What is the nature of Spirit? What purpose does suffering serve? If Spirit exists and is only Good, why do bad things happen?

Does it interest me that quantum mysteries are being scientifically revealed at this particular moment in time? Why right now, rather than a hundred years earlier or a hundred years later? What has been prepared in the mind of the collective whole of humanity that opens the way for these mysteries to be unveiled in this moment of time?

Does it interest me that the truths contained in the teachings from ancient mystery schools and age-old spiritual writings (e.g., Nag Hammadi Library) reveal advanced concepts. Concepts that are the foundation of modern day quantum physics? Does it interest me that mind and life is being revealed in a new way by science?

Does it interest me that the tool for the 21st century is consciousness? Does it interest me that the work of the 21st century is to *BE* conscious and that we are living in a pivotal moment in the history of humankind? Does it interest me that the work of the 21st century is to be interested in who I *BE* and how I am showing up as, in any given moment?

Does it interest me that Newtonian based concepts may be inadequate for interpreting 21st century understanding?
Does it interest me that people are beginning to see through their illusionary masks of self-doubt, fear, and feelings of inadequacy, and are moving into Self-Realization?

Does it interest me to discover that, at the quantum or -Q- level, which is a unified field of resonant energy, life and existence is not random and that everything is in relationship and is interconnected?

Does it interest me that, there is a heart-intelligence, a Gnosis-Cardia, and that research substantiates this concept; and that there is within me a still point, where the sound of Silence is deafening in its quiet.

Does it interest me that dedication to the spiritual path does not guarantee that my lessons will easy; it only guarantees only change?

Does it interest me that synchronistic events are a result of energies aligning to create "right" moments in what appears to be the occurrence of random happenings; and that quantum physics is revealing that everything is interconnected at the quantum level? So, how random can these events be?

Does it interest me that intuition; is a gift of insight and knowledge that leads to a deeper awakening, or understanding of a mystery hidden within my soul?

Does it interest me that new questions are birthing themselves, within me (right now), because I am open to the possibility of something new arising?

In the book, *"The Celestine Prophecy"*, the hero is on a personal quest of transformation. During his journey the hero meets a "wise being" who informs him that he needs to keep his questions in front of him and by doing so – the questions will answer themselves. Often, it is often in the asking of the question, that the answer arises voluntarily and so does an experience to fulfill it.

Once I began my own "heroes" journey, I initiated a search to find the answers to the questions that were stirring in my heart. I wanted to discover, what I considered to be valid answers to ethereal questions. I could justify the need to have my ethereal-type questions answered because after all, I had a Master's of Science in Nursing.

Science and research were my foundational building blocks; I was quantitative and analytical by nature. Thus, in accordance with my scientific background, I knew that if something was not measurable or determinable, it could not be considered valid. I was on a quest in search of ethereal wisdom, of the elusive and I wanted answers to that which was unanswerable – how "un-wisdom-like" is that?

In due course, I began to realize that the experience I was having, which looked like a hunger for more knowledge, was in actuality an interior call to awakening. The call was opening the way for my unearthing of information about the relationship between self and _S_elf. Eventually, I began to realize that my discoveries did not need the validation of scientific proof. I realized that to *BE* in deep relationship with the Mystery, to dance with Its questions, and to sit at Its edge, was more valid as a research, investigative, and explorative method than any *official* scientific query. After many years and many spiritual experiences, a shift has taken place within me and I know that answers are not necessary. What is important, however, to my soul's evolution is that I *BE* willing to dance at the edge of mystery and observe how comfortable I am in my own skin as questions and experiences arise? This is the true north of the mystery experience.

I realize that I will never have the all answers; in fact, it is clear to me that in the big scheme of things I know nothing. Thus, I no longer seek to prove or answer anything. Being present to the energy of moment and being interested in what that energy wants to reveal energetically to me and through me, is more important. Being aware of revelations such as, synchronistic (synchro-divinity) events stirring around me or the slight, but perceptible, intuitive "nudges", "hits", and awareness' arising within me – are just a few of the glories that I desire and live for now. Centered in this awareness, life is much easier and more grace-filled. I look back now and wonder just how loud the Universe was laughing at my antics, determinedness, blessed ignorance, and naivety as I "tried to control" my own life.

Note: Throughout this book, the Sacred is referred to as the Sacred Source of Life as God, One, Source, No-Thing, Universe, Universal Presence, Mystery, Self, -O-, etc. Please use words that speak to your heart.

Meandering through the pages of this book be open to new ideas and awareness'. Be awake and alert to synchronistic (synchro-divinity) events arise across all the various venues of your life and the intuitive hits that arise from within. Be alert to and be willing to follow the cosmic threads that energetically pull you along the path. Consciously be with that which are learning in both your personal and professional life. See your work environment as a sacred space where you have the privilege to put into practice the living reality of that "which you *BE!*"

Chapter 2
"Y.E.S. – Your Energetic Source

> *"The universe had dealt me a hand and now it was*
> *time for me to choose how I wanted to play it.*
> *If I was going to say, "YES",*
> *to a greater possibility revealing itself,*
> *then I had to change my attitudes and behaviors.*
> *I realized that in order for this to happen*
> *I would have to surrender all of my expectations,*
> *all of my frustrations, and make room for ...*
> *something greater to emerge."*[11]
> --Toni G. Boehm

Life at its True Core is a Mystery and a "YES!"

> *"Observe the wonders as they occur around you.*
> *Do not claim them. Feel the artistry*
> *moving through, and be silent".*
> --Rumi[12]

Life at its true core is a mystery, the essence of the field is a mystery; yet, whether we are conscious of it or not, we have already said, "YES!" to participating in the mystery. When I speak before audiences and mention the idea of "dancing at the edge of mystery" a stir created that is palpable.

People are interested in this concept. They respond as if this concept is unfamiliar to them; yet, do we all not dance at the edge of mystery in every moment of our lives?

In every moment that we wait for the arising of the next breath; in every moment that we willingly surrender to that invisible something and trust that it will beat our heart again; in every moment such as these and more, are we not dancing at the edge of mystery? The answer is, "YES, we are!"

The Evolutionary Pulse and Sacred Dance of "YES"

At a workshop we were co-facilitating in Nashville, Tennessee, my dear friend, Andrew Harvey, shared a story about a petroglyph, a rock drawing, which he had seen in the desert. This rock drawing touched his soul and spoke to his heart. The following is my summation of what he shared about the drawing and our combined thoughts on its relationship to the idea of The Power of BE! and the energetic "YES! of the Universe that life pulses through each of us:

---

[11] Boehm, Toni G. *The Power of "YES!".* Inner Visioning Press. Greenwood, MO. pg. 5
[12] Barks, Coleman. *The Poetry of Rumi Journal.* Brush Dance Publications. Sausalito, CA.

The gift of the rock drawing was left by the indigenous people, known as the Anasazi's. It is an ancient picture drawn on a vast, molten copper-colored rock. The drawing depicts stick figures, perhaps a man and a woman, dancing with what appears to be their arms outstretched above their head. The figures are positioned in a dance of praise and affirmation. They are so consumed by the sacred energy of the Universe that Its power is being expressed as lightning and as spirals flowing forth from the soles of their feet. These lightning flashes and spirals are streaming out in all directions, as chaotic bursts of electrified Light-Energy that cannot be contained.

It would appear that the figures are dancing at the edge of mystery and that they are consumed with the rhythm and energy of the pulsating "YES" of life as it moves through them. It is apparent that they have become aware of the great mystery of the sacred "YES" energy that lives and breathes them. "YES" is revealed and released through them as a surging and pulsating passion coursing through every cell of their being.

In this dazzling reflection of the creative power of the universal "YES", this evolutionary pulse, blazing streams of energy pour forth from them as fire and this fire flashes out through the cellular structure of their bodies. They are consumed by the "YES".

With one gesture of "YES", these beings are offering themselves to the Universal Energy and power, known as God; and they are doing this wholly and completely, and with great abandon. It is apparent that the "YES" energy possesses them and that this same "YES" transfigures them into a state of Oneness with the Source of the sacred power. Offering themselves to their God, they dance at the edge of mystery in a state of divine bliss.

Dancing with un-abandoned pleasure, surrendered to the moment, they know not where their dance will lead. They only know that dance they must and dance they do; dancing with a grand gesture of "YES", they open their whole self to being filled by the field of energy surrounding them, by an energy that is greater than themselves, yet which expresses Itself through them as the Self of BEing.

Dancing at the edge of mystery "YES" calls them and compels them to give their selves as an offering to the One. This conscious act of surrender sends forth a powerful, but silent, energetic vibration into the field of universal Substance. This resonance with the universal energy of life's "YES" co-creates a mighty force that can only go forth to imprint upon the substance of the universal field and call forth into being the deepest desires of the their hearts, as it fuses them in oneness with the One Energy.

The picture reveals that it is the sacred act of surrender that invites the energy of the creative "YES" into their midst, and it also reveals that their posture is one of total freedom for having made that decision. This paradox is a vital part of the mystery of the dance of the creative "YES" – the act of both total surrender and un-abandoned freedom taking place in the same moment, at the same edge.

It is apparent that their surrender is not an act of sacrifice; on the contrary, inherent in seeing their posture of surrender, one can feel simultaneously that this act of surrender is made through a sense of freedom to *BE* one with the One and this opens their hearts to a direct transmission of Divine Love.

A person looking on can see with the naked eye, even hundreds of centuries later, how their "YES" is creating a joining of the body, heart, spirit, and soul into the Oneness of *BE*ing. A coming together of Source and Power, mind and heart, light and dark, body and soul, spirit and matter, surrender and freedom, and masculine and feminine – in what could be construed as a cosmic orgasm of the universe.

What is utterly amazing is that this power of "YES" lives in the depths of your being and longs for you to unite with it; to unite with the true energy of who you *BE*. The question is; "Are you ready to say "YES" to its movement through you?"

A "Mystery" Practice: The Sacred Dance of "YES"

You are invited to take a moment – in the privacy of your home, in the woods, at the water's edge, or wherever you choose that calls to the deep essence of your heart – to come into the Presence of the Universal "YES". Once you find the perfect spot, stand with your legs set slightly apart for balance and take three deep cleansing breaths. Breath in deeply and then breath out – releasing, releasing, releasing.

Stretch forth your arms and bring them above your head in an act that is a conscious offering to the "YES" of your being. Stretch forth your arms and like the Anasazi couple, be willing to "dance at the edge of mystery". Invite both the attitude of surrender and freedom to reside within you, in this moment.

Stand, not as a victim with the burdens of life weighing you down, but stand-up straight, with your arms outstretched over your head creating the "Y" as a symbol of the universal "YES". Stand as one willing to participate in the sacredness of the divine dance of Life. As you stretch forth your arms, you *BE* the 'living' body prayer of the energy of the creative "YES".

Begin to speak your "YES" into the universal Substance. Speak your "YES" softly, at first, letting it gather power and conviction. Allow the energy to grow as the sound of your "YES" increases in volume. Speak it aloud, now, with an intensity of power and conviction and with an intention that reveals that you are willing to dance at the edge of mystery – come what may!

Continue to speak your "YES" into the forming Substance of the universe; speak your "YES" over and over and over and over and over – do not be self-conscious, just *BE* willing. The universal substance is waiting to respond to the vibration and power of the movement of your spoken word throughout its living body of energy.

Speak your "YES", 20, 30, 40, or 100 times or more; until you feel Its power moving throughout your mind, body, and soul. Surrender into Its energy, release and let go, be drawn into Its Vibration. Allow the universal "YES" to begin to resonant within your being. You will know when you have surrendered into freedom. Let "YES" consume you. You will feel it in every cell of your being when you have released yourself into the One. Have no fear for Absolute Love will never harm you.

Is there something that you would like to say "YES" to? Whatever it may be, speak it out into the universal substance, now! Let it make its imprint in the quantum field of energy that is vibrating around you.

Having spoken your desire into and onto universe substance, in a conscious act of surrender, release what it is that you think you want and invite your heart to call forth that which is for your highest good and that which is ready to make itself known through you. Again, have no fear about this releasing process – for Absolute Love will never harm you.

Once you are complete, and have finished speaking "YES" for the co-creation of your transformation and growth, dedicate your "YES" to an opportunity for sacred service to the universe. You may choose to dedicate your "YES" to the uplifting of global consciousness; to the elimination of abuse towards children, women, and/or animals; to awakening the consciousness of humankind to Divine Love; to World Peace, to finding a cure for a disease, or ... whatever it is that is moving in your heart in the moment.

This is the time for "YES"! Let us bring the energy of the creative "YES" into the world, NOW! Not just for ourselves but for all sentient beings.

After you are complete, take a moment to ground your experience in the 3D realm by journaling about your "YES" experience. What do you notice?

"What Do You Want to Experience in Your Life?"

Do you know what you want to experience in and for your life? If you do, are you actually receiving what it is that you are asking for? Does it seem that you often ask for one thing and receive another? Do you understand why this happens? If asking for one thing and receiving something different is a continuing pattern in your life, be prepared for change!

Working consciously with the energy of "YES" will attract back to you that which you have sent forth as a dominant thought, want, or desire. The key idea here is "dominant thought".

Our dominant thoughts and feelings determine the outcome of our intentions. You cannot affirm that you want to experience or manifest this or that and then follow it up with all sorts of bad vibes, negative feelings and thoughts or reasons, or excuses for why it will not possibly come true.

This negative spewing is called Monkey Mind Chatter (MMC) and MMC sabotages our good efforts.

> e.g., We affirm: "I am a successful sales person. I am in service to all who come for my (goods). I reach   by   ." Then we follow that wonder-filled affirmation with MMC such as; "Well, this could be true if   ; if Susie or Don don't continue to be top sellers...; if I only had a few years education; if I...

We continue to fuel this MMC with more thoughts and more thoughts and more reasons; until what we have actually imprinted upon the fabric of the substance of reality is a negative scenario and not a positive one.

Are you aware that it takes five positive affirmations to overcome one negative one – so be careful what thoughts and feelings you hold and express!

When we throw in all those negative thoughts we dissipate all the positive energy we had previously built up through our affirmation/s. The universe returns our dominant thoughts to us as our manifestations or outcomes.

Being conscious of what it is we say, after we speak our desire into the universe, is of utmost importance. To work consciously with our thoughts requires that we embark upon a journey into the realm of self-discovery; a.k.a., self-observation, self-awareness, self-reflection, and self-honesty.

Self-discovery involves detecting and then shedding the "old beliefs" that no longer serve us in life. Through this act of unmasking and shedding, we realize that we are the only person responsible for our life and that we alone have the power to shift and shape the conditions of our life.

The energy of "YES" lives within us and desires to give us our highest good when we consciously participate with it. "YES" is an attractor for the flow of creative, universal energy – what we create depends upon our intentions, words, and actions. When we say, "YES" to something and then follow it up with enough "No's", our "No" becomes our new "YES". Does this interest you?

As preparation for the journey into a deeper understanding of the workings of the power of "YES", please take a moment and reflect upon the following question:

"What do I really want to experience in my life and how am I consciously working to bring that about – or not?"

Please journal your response.

'Y.E.S.' is Your Energetic Source!

Do you recall the shampoo commercial in which a woman was in the shower washing her hair and having an organic experience? Do you remember what the words were that she was using to express the intensity of that moment for her? She was ecstatically repeating, "YES!" "YES!" "YES!"

While we watched that commercial we could feel the intensity of that woman's experience; we could feel her resounding "YES". That "YES" had an effect on us as the listener. Whether we wanted to buy the shampoo or not, was secondary to the feeling that we walked away with from having been a voyeur in the hair-washer's experience. We knew she was completely involved in her experience and we felt her excitement. It left no doubt in our minds that she was involved in a great hair washing experience and that and she was enjoying the experience immensely.

What if we could hold that kind of intensity of intention with the ideas that we desire to manifest in our lives? What would happen? What would or could we co-create?

Personally, I have a love affair with the word, 'YES.' I have always felt that the word "YES" had a cosmic meaning that we as a species had not yet fully understood. In my book, *The Spiritual Intrapreneur*, there is a definition for the word "YES" given in the form of an acronym "Y.E.S." stands for: *Your Empowerment System*

"YES" acts as an empowering agent for good when we speak positive words aloud or silently and combine them with an intensity of feeling (as we discovered in doing the last Mystery Experience). "YES" combined with positive intentions and intensity of feelings is recognized by the Universe as approval, as an endorsement to go forth and do the work that we have sent it forth to do.

Our "YES", in whatever form we send it forth, is imprinted into and onto a universal substance that acts as a magnet of attraction. This magnet of attraction draws back to us that which we have set forth as our intention.

Thus, through the activity of the creative "YES", we open the way for the universe to support us in receiving our intended outcomes. The question is: "What are you actually sending forth as an intention?"

"YES", is a creative energy that lives within each one of us and "YES" desires to go forth and co-create the highest and best for our lives. "YES" is a statement of faith that says, "I know I can do this." "I know this can happen to me." "I know that I can realize my dream." "I am somebody." "I have skills." "I am worthy."

However, to take an active part in this creative energy of "YES" we have to be willing to take authentic action. This means that we speak our "YES" into the universe with positive conviction – like the woman in the shower commercial shampooing her hair, totally involved with her experience – we, too, must hold our intention with conviction of purpose.

With an intensity of positive feelings and belief that says, "What I speak will come into manifestation." Our intentions are also reinforced when we do not permit any type of short-circuiting through thoughts of negativity and fear.

While we consciously, hold our convictions, beliefs, and intentions about what we are sending forth, a stream of thought-energy is created. This stream of positive thought-energy imprints upon the invisible fabric of reality composed of universal substance.

This substance is all around us and holds within it the power to change and transform the conditions of our life. It awaits our willingness to participate through our "YES."

Upon reflection, after writing, *The Spiritual Intrapreneur*, I would now expand my concept of "YES" and say that "Y.E.S." is not only *Your Empowerment System*, it is also: *"Your Energetic Source"*

Your Energetic Source, a 21st century concept. Quantum physics is revealing that we are connected to this energy source, not just on occasion, as when we go into prayer, but all the time. Determining factors as to how powerfully (or deeply) we feel this energetic connection includes:

How we work with the universal energy while we are imprinting it upon the fabric of substance.

How clear or transparent we are, personally
(Refer to chapter on Shadow-Dancing)

When we work to imprint our intentions upon the fabric of substance we do so with clarity of intention that we are: affirming, inviting, knowing, positive, free from negativity/fear, and non-emotionally attached to the outcome. Clarity of intention, along with an abiding conviction in what we are creating, aligns us consciously with the universal energy and supports our ability to co-create with it.

One reason I respect the word "YES" so much is that "YES" is tied to the beginning of everything. In the beginning something had to say, 'YES.' Whether it was a divine Being saying "YES" to the creation of Being or, our parents consenting to be at the same place in the same moment; something, some universal energy said "YES", to a creative experience happening in that moment. A "YES" or consent was imprinted upon universal substance and the substance responded – this is how creation works.

When we become aware that there is a great manifestation working power that lives within us and that its energy desires to co-create with us as a blazing, radiant, passionate, intense, and potent energy – why would we not consciously participate with it to co-create a better world for our families, all sentient beings, and ourselves?

Be aware that engaging with the creative aspects of "YES" will ultimately tear asunder the veils of illusion and negative beliefs that we hold about everything and everyone in our lives, certainly including ourselves. "YES" will transform us!

A "Mystery" Practice: a -Q- Vision: How Big Do You Dare to Dream?

> *"...We design our lives through the power of our choices.*
> *We feel most helpless when we've made choices by default."* [13]
> --Richard Bach

As you participate in this appreciate inquiry experience, stay open to possibility. Answer the questions without any concern about not being seen as humble, for in this moment you are to play big.

*Imagine it is five years from now and miracles have occurred in your life; everything that you have put forth as a goal, desire, or intention has manifested. Visualize yourself at a banquet, about to be honored. You have been requested to share a few words about the attainment of your goals and successes. You have also been asked to thank all the people who assisted you in making your -Q- vision, goals and dreams a reality.

> *"Mentally enter into your dream, mentally do*
> *what you would actually do, were it physically true.*
> *You will discover that dreams are realized not by the rich,*
> *but by the imagination...change your imagining...*
> *change the facts."* [14]
> – Neville

Take your journal or a piece of paper and list everything (dare to imagine big) you can imagine that has happened to you over those five years to make your dreams a reality. Be sure to include all those persons who assisted you in creating these miracles in your life. (These do not have to be people you know or currently in your life, they can be people you want to attract to you. e.g., I met a man at the grocery who asked if I was interested in job...)

Note: Although doing this may seem a little far-fetched, I can assure you that things like this happen. *If you can dream, you can achieve it.*

The purpose of this exercise is to get your creative juices flowing and beginning to imprint your good onto the fabric of substance.

---

[13] Bach, Richard. *One.* pg.98
[14] Neville. *The Law and the Promise.* pg.15

A Cosmic 2x4 Experience

*"Though we seem to be sleeping there is an inner wakefulness
that directs the dream, and will eventually startle us back
to the truth of who we are."*
--Rumi [15]

Throughout history, humankind has utilized oral tradition, chants, wall drawings, and other venues to share their legends, tales, practices, and traditions. Of all of these venues, oral tradition, is the most popular mode of expression. People get involved in story on a cellular level; because stories move us through the feeling level. Narrative accounts that chronicle our journey through the mysterious passages of life's experiences serve to share the essence of who we are, individually and collectively, with others.

Telling one's own personal story, sharing the personal parts of ones life is seen as an authentic action (AA); however, it does not mean that we have the right to emotionally vomit all over people. Authentic action arises out of having made peace with a situation, person, or experience and then being able to share your story with a sense of non-negative emotional attachment. It is with this intention that I share my story with you.

A few years ago I found myself in the midst of an experience that I refer to as a time of dancing at the edge of mystery. It began when the universe clobbered me over the head with its proverbial Cosmic 2x4; it happened both literally and figuratively. I had fallen and hit my head and that fall resulted in a mild traumatic brain injury. During the five-month period that followed, I had a loss of my short-term memory. Full recovery took about 18 months. I remember the exact moment that it felt like the "fog" lifted. The injury, however, became a catalyst that led to my taking a leave of absence from my place of employment and pulling back from being in service to work that I loved.

Initially, this was a difficult and tumultuous time for me. Everything was new and everything was strange. The loss of memory was frustrating and I was angry. Additionally, I felt sorry for myself and I felt frightened. Not going to work was difficult. I had worked continuously for nearly 40 years, without ever taking much more than a few weeks off at any given time.

After about two weeks of engaging in this self-absorbed, potentially self-destructive behavior; during meditation, I had an epiphany, which I will describe in detail in Chapter 6. For now, it is suffice to say that negative energy permeated all I did and after this epiphany experience, I was able to "see" and "read" energy with a greater sense of clarity and understanding. I "saw" myself clearly. I saw how I was acting and *reacting* to what was happening.

[15] Barks, Coleman. *The Poetry of Rumi Journal.* Brush Dance Publications. Sausalito, CA.

All the chaos, frustration, weariness, concern, and madness that I was exhibiting was revealed through short clips of pictures that arose before the screen of my mind's eye. When this happened, I gasped. I felt horrified that I would behave like this. After all, I knew better than this. Surely, I had learned, over my many years of spiritual study, more than this. How could I be heaping guilt, shame, and blame upon myself; using shoulda, coulda, woulda to provide justification and comfort for myself?

I had been engaging with monkey mind chatter (remember that MMC is that incessant, negative chatter in our mind that tries desperately to get us to believe what it is saying is true) and it was time to stop! So I did! I stopped, took a deep breath, and I looked honestly at all my reactive behaviors. I saw how they were affecting my life and my healing process. I became quiet and I listened, and I listened some more. I went within and waited for Spirit to guide me into a more authentic-type of action.

My guidance told me to start journaling about my experience and to stop asking, "Why did this happen to me?" I began to think in terms of asking myself 'right' questions. Right questions are those questions we ask that move us into new frames of awareness and that elicit positive responses and actions.

Was it easy? No! Was it difficult? No! It was what I needed to do I knew it and I did it. I knew was dancing at the edge of mystery and that now I was being asked to step into the unknown and trust that whatever I needed to move forward would be there to support me.

I began to ask myself the same questions that I pose to you throughout this book. "What do I really want to experience in my life?" Do I want to sit around moping, feeling sorry for myself, and fearful that I will never be able to remember anything again? No! It wasn't what I wanted – then why was I creating it? The universe had dealt me a hand and now it was time for me to choose how I wanted to play it. If I was going to say "YES" to greater possibility revealing itself, then I had to shift my perceptions, attitudes, behaviors, and actions.

As I began to ask myself "right" questions, thoughts arose. I realized that I wanted not just a physical healing but also a healing that would be an uplifting for my soul and move me towards greater spiritual growth. I realized that in order for that growth to happen, I would have to surrender all my expectations around healing. I had to surrender into the idea that a Higher Power knew what was best for my life and for my soul growth.

In my heart, I knew that an invitation was being extended to me and that I was being called to step into the dance of mystery and to participate at a level that had never before been asked of me. I was invited to surrender everything that was happening to me unto a Higher Nature and this act of surrender contained an infinite number of possibilities. One possibility was that perhaps my memory was not going to return and I would have to be all right with that.

Yes, you read that correctly – surrender, means surrender! I had to surrender all my ideas of the perfect outcome and dance at the edge of mystery while the right and perfect outcome arose from what it was that my soul needed next for its growth. I would have to *BE* peace – to *BE* surrender. I also realized that my own Higher Nature was asking me, to dance at the edge of mystery and to wait in the unknown for the unfolding of the next step of my life.

I said, *"YES! I will dance at the edge of mystery. I will allow the Unseen and the Unknown to work Itself through me."* Having said "YES" to engaging fully with the unknown, breathing in and breathing out was all I could do in those next moments as I sat and awaited the next step.

So, sit I did, laugh I did, contemplate my navel I did, walk I did, read I did, rest I did, pray I did, and dance I did. But I did not worry, I let that all go.

Suddenly, the creative force of the Unknown began to make Itself known to me and through me. I began to write as if someone else was guiding my thoughts and hands. What came through me I call *Soul Searching's*. *Soul Searching's*, in the form of odes and poems started to flow forth, each one a reflection of my struggles, my fears, my hopes, my strengths, my healing, my dreams; each a reflection of where I was in consciousness during this transition and transformation process.

What I did not realize, immediately, was that each time I wrote an ode or poem I was sending a healing message throughout my cellular structure. As each one came, they peeled away a layer of unconscious muck and mire – old stuff that had been running my life for years. As the writings turned into a collection, each one with a new idea, I realized that they were part of my healing process. So, heal I did! "YES!" "YES!" "YES!"

When I look back on the situation, I now know that I had many choices, many routes that I could have taken; but I had to make the choice as to the one I wanted to imprint upon the substance of the universe. Choice was the key and intention was the key hole that my choices had to fit into, perfectly, or they would not work.

I made a choice to dance at the edge of mystery and *BE* peace and *BE* surrender. I created an intention, which was to live life with a sense of spaciousness, grace, and ease. Then every choice I made after that I consciously made sure it was congruent with that original choice and subsequent intention.

Sitting in mystery, the authentic action that became clear to take as my next step, was for me to retire from the traditional grind of daily, organizational work and to renew and replenish myself through other venues. I knew by making that choice I was making a choice that was going to take me to another edge of mystery. And it would require that I be comfortable there for quite a while. The choice was and is the right one for this time in my life. I live in peace and joy and all my needs are abundantly met!

A deep understanding of the power of "YES" evolved for me out of that cosmic 2x4 experience. "YES" is an attractor for the creative and positive, universal energy. Each day my understanding of "YES" deepens its roots in the fertile soil of my soul and through that deepening process; I came to write the book, *The Power of* "YES!"

This cosmic 2x4 experience, however, was only a preparatory experience akin to kindergarten, for what was to come next into our lives. Within a few months after the "fog" lifting experience, my husband received a diagnosis of "terminal" disease; with less than a few months to live. This time we were prepared, "YES" permeated our consciousness and we walked through the experience with grace, faith, and knowing that "nothing can disturb the calm peace of our soul." It has taken almost two years, but as of this writing he is in remission, full of vitality, walking again and as always, in great spirits. "YES!"

Yes, shift happens in life; however the key is to always be 'consciously' prepared to say "YES"; "YES" to life, "YES" to change, "YES" to stirrings, "YES" to forward movement, "YES" to working with the BE! Building Blocks of consciousness, and "YES" to dancing at the edge of mystery.

A "Mystery" Practice: Igniting the -Q- Spark

This experience is about staying open to possibility and to seeing the greater potential that resides within you. As you answer the following questions do so without any concern about being humble, this is a moment for you to play big.

* Think about a time when you experienced a positive flow of energy, when you felt one with the -Q- field. There was power moving through an experience or situation that you were involved with; a time you were in the -Q- flow! A time when you received "kudo's" for something you did or for a project you helped with. With great clarity, remember not only the experience, but also the feeling of the experience.

*What was the experience?
*What were you doing and who were you engaged with?
*What personal resources did you bring to the experience that made it so fulfilling?
*What is it that you most value about yourself, for having participated in the experience?
*What did it feel like to receive all that positive energy?
*Where, in your body do you feel the expression of those positive feelings, when you speak about them?
*What knowledge and/or values did the experience leave you with?

The feeling that you felt as you recalled that positive experience is a spark that you can flame into a blazing fire of authentic action. Feeling into that energetic memory, create an authentic action around an goal or idea that you have wanted to bring into manifestation. Work consciously with your new go/ authentic action to re-create a similar positive outcome. Take a sweet, small step, nothing big at first, for authentic actions do not have to be big or overwhelming. In fact, when goals are on target they should bring joy into your life for having participated with them. Start with a small step/goal that fits into a bigger life intention or goal and when that is completed create another small step and before you know it, you will have accomplished something big!

My goal is to.... by .... !

A "Mystery" Practice: Creating a Mission Statement for My Life

"I am a midwife for the birthing
of the soul's remembrance."
--Toni G. Boehm

This personal life mission statement I created over 15 years ago and it remains the benchmark for all I participate in and with, today. It is about who I am and it is what I do in life. In all I do and in all I undertake or say "yes" to, I measure the value of the activity against this statement (along with my own core values). By doing this I can see if the activity resonates with and/or aligns with who I say I am and what I want to do in life.

To start this experience take a few minutes to be still, get quiet, and practice interior listening. Consciously bring and hold your attention in your heart space. After a period of quiet begin to gently ask yourself the following questions: "Who am I?" "What is my life's mission or purpose?" "How can I best serve in life and in the universe?"

Remember, we are dancing at the edge of mystery, moving into the state of *BE*! Thus, answers are not our focus. We are willing to allow these questions have their way with our heart, and to wait for what desires to come forth into expression to be revealed.

Create Your Own Life Vision, Mission and Purpose

Part I   My Life's Vision, Mission and Purpose:
I am a ...
I creatively express ...

Part II   Natural Qualities that I Am:
Generous   Attentive   Aware   Centered   Honest   Others

Part III   Talents and Abilities I use in Sacred Service:
Healer, Listener, Singer, Songwriter, Humorist, Prayer, Others

Part IV   Creating Your Life Vision, Mission and Purpose
Statement:
I am/I:
I use the qualities of):
In service to :

Example:
I am a channel of creative expression using all I am and do for the uplifting of the universe.

> *Take a piece of paper and make your own statement.*
> *Start your sentence with I am or I.*
> *As above add your unique qualities, talents and abilities.*
> *Create Your Own Personal Life Mission or Purpose Statement*

Example:
"I am a midwife for the birthing of the soul's remembrance."

Chapter 3
Shadow-Dancing and En'lighten'ment

*"Wholeness...is not achieved
by cutting off a portion of one's being,
But by integrating the contraries."*
--Carl Jung

En'lighten'ment: What does it mean?

"Enlightenment is an increase of consciousness."
--Carl Jung

As we are willing to shine the light on our shadow aspects and to face those shadows we free up, bound, limited, and negative energy; and we open the way for more "light" or energy to shine through consciousness. In his book, *"Alchemical Studies"*, Carl Jung refers to enlightenment in this way:
*"... the light shines within,
it can be understood as illumination
which wholeness brings.
Enlightenment is an increase of consciousness."*[16]

En'lighten'ment then is the release of light or energy into consciousness. This light comes from having cleaned up or cleared up our toxic beliefs and their companions, projections. It is these toxic beliefs and projections that have blocked the light from shining through consciousness and thus, have created deterrents to the expression of wholeness.

The Void Of Forgetfulness

*"I have cast __fire__ upon the world,
and look, I'm guarding it until it blazes."*[17]
--Gospel of Thomas; The Nag Hammadi Library

As was stated in the story of the little blue planet, humankind (collectively and individually) has forgotten what we came here to learn about who we are on a soul level through life experiences, in order that we can return to the conscious awareness of *BE.*

Because we are unaware of our true purpose, we often feel out of balance, that something is missing, or a part of us is lost. There are many theories on the why's of these feelings, but for now we will go with the idea that on an unconscious level we have forgotten who we *BE*/truly are and we are on a

16 Jung, Carl. *Collected Works 13, Alchemical Studies.* Princeton/Bollinger. New York. pg.. 85
17 Patterson, Stephen and Meyer, Marvin (Trans.). *The Nag Hammadi Library.* Gnostic Society. Logion 10

search to remember and to regain our balance. However, instead of searching within for what we perceive as the "missing elements" we look to the outer world in hopes of finding a sense of fulfillment, joy, and balance.

What happens when we search outside ourselves for anything? We end up looking for "our sense of being/wholeness/ completion/love" in all the wrong places. We go in search of that ubiquitous something, thinking it "lives" outside of ourselves, in someone else or something else in this material world. This intense pursuit leads us to live our lives from what I call the "v*oid of forgetfulness*".

The "v*oid of forgetfulness*" lives in and through the power of the subconscious mind; the subconscious mind is a repository of our experiences, it is pivotal and can look to Truth/Spirit or to sense perception – depending upon our choices. Perceptions drive our thoughts and influence our interpretations of what we see, feel, think, and how we "show up" in the world. The perceptions that we derive from our experiences, drive our choices when we are unconscious.

Our perceptions, since they are formed from energetic memories of past experiences, are a false indicator of what is truly real. Perceptions are a collection of error thoughts and feelings, created from erroneous beliefs of what we think happened to us and that then get stored in the subconscious mind, to used as recall for protection. These perceptions get triggered when we are confronted with certain types of experiences in life that we perceive as dangerous, fearful, etc.

Perceptions often tell us that we are incomplete, stupid, not smart enough, not good enough, empty-headed, don't have enough, aren't loveable enough, worthy enough ...

When we feel we are not enough ... it is like an unquenchable thirst. We cannot get enough of (fill in the blank) to quench the sense of emptiness that the perception engenders. We cannot fill the void that is created by what we feel is missing in us.

In order to feel better about who we are, we try to fill this "void or empty place" with things, toys, money, a need for piousness, righteousness, manipulation, or this, that, and the other. Whatever it is that we choice to fill the void, it will however never be enough! In fact, the more we try to fill the void, the bigger the void gets, for it *craves* more to fill its unquenchable thirst.

In pursuing our need to fill the empty space we enlarge the "*void of forgetfulness*" and we become what I refer to as:

"*a-holics*"; booze-a-holics, rage-a-holics, food-a-holics, sex-a-holics, drug-a-holics, shop-a-holics, control-a-holics ...

Can you see from that list of words that "a-holic" as a suffix tends to connote that a negative behavior is associated with the word to which it is connected? "A-holic" behaviors do not fulfill anything; they are a result of being in the *void of forgetfulness*.

"A-hol-ic!" If this suffix were broken down into syllables with each syllable given a definition then an "A-holi-c" would be:

"A" — as a prefix to a word or syllable indicates or means without, from or, opposite to.

"Hol" — is a play on holy and whole; connoting the Truth of who we are as sacred beings – whole and holy.

"Ic" — having the behaviors or characteristic of, and associated with.

"Aholic" one who is without the knowledge of the Truth of their Being and thus, uses an external substance, means, or behavior to try to fill the void they are experiencing from the lack of this knowledge.

Thus, when we are living in the *void of forgetfulness*, we are living the opposite of our intended state of being. We are living without knowing the essence of the holy or whole person that we *BE*.

We have forgotten this truth, and our attitudes and behaviors reflect this forgetting. Forgetting tends to send us out to look in all the wrong places for the answers to our deepest longings, longings that we think will be fulfilled from outside stimuli, but in reality can only be fulfilled from turning within to find our true Self.

When the alcoholic decides that they have taken their "last drink", this decision is made because something within them has stirred a remembrance of a truth of who they truly are; whether, at the moment, they consciously realize it or not.

A friend of mine shared that at one point in her life she was what people would call a falling down drunk, alcoholic. One day she went to her closet to get a pair of shoes and as she started to pull on the light cord, she felt a "bolt of electricity" go through her. She had an epiphany about her drinking habits and walked out of the closet, changed! What happened? It was a synchro-divinity moment, for on a soul level she was ready and willing to claim her sobriety!

It represented her having said, "YES!", to something of which she was not completely aware of, yet. She had interiorly said, "YES!" to change and the perfect moment unfolded for the expressing of that "YES!"

Thus, the metaphor of walking into a dark closet, turning on a light, and having an epiphany was not a coincidence; it was an alignment of the –Q-field. This alignment is also referred as synchronicity or synchro-divinity..

Her willingness to enter into the mystery came about as she embraced her fears and remembered the truth of who she *BE*!. Because of that remembrance, her life was changed. She made, in that moment, a conscious choice.

Her choice was to begin to take an authentic action; to align with the characteristics of her "holiness", or wholeness, rather than her a-hol-ic-ness (alcoholic behaviors). She released the "a", the attachment to the without "stuff" and turned within. She moved from "the a-holic" to "the (w) holic," one who remembers their (w) holiness.

She remembered that the "*void of forgetfulness*" is never filled or satisfied with things outside of her – not even another drink! She remembered the truth that the feeling in the midst of the "*void of forgetfulness*" is not a sense of emptiness, but a deep longing to return to Love. From finding this *love of self* she experienced a quantum transformation. My friend is now a minister and very content within herself and in her new life.

It's Dark Down Here; Does Any One Have a Light?

"Darkness gives birth to light;
... what is unconscious becomes conscious
in the form of a living process of growth...
In this way the union of consciousness and life take place."[18]
--Carl Jung

As we consciously choose to embark upon the spiritual journey – the mythic hero's quest – we, at some point, will face our shadow-aspects. True inner work is initiated when we consciously confront or care-front the "shadow-aspects" of self.

Self-revelation is a requirement as we move from unconscious beings attached to and steeped in the things of matter to – a 21st century creative partners and energy beings – steeped in the conscious awareness of who we truly are at our deepest level, consciously aware of the energy that surrounds us.

The invitation to be a 21st century energetic being is a movement in consciousness that calls us into deeper levels of conviction; no longer practicing and seeking but moving into the awareness of *BE*.

BE the presence of -- *BE* faith, *BE* surrender, *BE* trust, *BE* non-judgment, *BE* non-attachment, *BE* non-resistance, *BE* integrity, *BE* the meditative state, and *BE now!*

18
  Jung, Carl; Collected Works 13, Alchemical Studies; Princeton/Bollinger, New York; pg. 24

Rely only on the inner awareness that arises or emerges from a Higher Source within and that guides and directs every movement, on a moment-to-moment basis.

As 21st century creative partners our reliance is no longer only on Newtonian mental-type processes. We live from a new matrix of information that holds a more transparent thought-energy and is intuitive by nature. However, in order for clarity and transparency of thought to present itself, we must clean-up the "sludge", energy leaks and muck lurking in the sub-conscious mind. Carl Jung in his *Collected Works* shares these words:

> *"One does not become __enlightened__ by imaging figures of light but by making the darkness [the unconscious] conscious."*

Confrontation and acceptance of our shadow-side is touted as the cornerstone of inner work. There is a whole internal environment available to us that is rich with guidance and intuition, and it arises from a universal matrix of 'downloadable' information that comes through being the transparency and "seeing" with clarity. This information is available, as we clean-up our sludge and shadows and grow in the conscious awareness of and connection to Source.

Spiritual teachers throughout the centuries have taught about this sacred connection. They have performed what has appeared to be miracles when they were simply in alignment with a "higher" matrix of information.

Our work, in the evolution of consciousness is to "rid" ourselves of the distractions that have become more interesting to us; distractions that keep us mired in the "muck" continuing the illusion of being unconscious. "Rid" does not mean "forcibly extract". It means consciously allowing love to lead the way to a deeper uncovering of who we are as conscious vibrational-beings. Debbie Ford, in her seminal work, *The Dark Side of the Light Chasers* says:

> *"...you cannot undo what you have done, but you can clear the negative effects of your experiences."*

The question that naturally arises is, "How do we clear our negative experiences?" "How do we clear ourselves and become transparent?" For many, it begins with a simple conviction and statement of "YES" to living life differently. This desire to engage with life in a new way, eventually leads to the door of awakening; to knowing and understanding more about self and Self/Source. By asking the question, "Who am I?" we are eventually led by Source or Spirit or Soul, into the depths of our subconscious mind, where the deeper work is done.

The subconscious mind is also known as, the "playground" of the mind. In actuality, a playground is an apt name for the subconscious. The subconscious mind is the place where our scripts, egoic patterns, self-identities, false beliefs, shadow issues, and all of the different masks we have played with and hidden behind throughout our lives, reside. These false identities came forth for us to use, as we acted out our various unconscious roles (and perhaps conscious at times), wearing well-crafted masks.

Shadow-work is no easy task, it takes a willingness and a stick-to-it-iveness to begin to differentiate the false from the true. To uncover the reasons that we wear our various masks and hide behind all the different aspects of our persona and layers of mis-information that inform us about life and its experiences – is quite a job – and it is not for the faint of heart.

There is within each of us in consciousness layers of muck (false beliefs, personas, perceptions, masks, etc.) that we must sift and shift through and then clear, in order to claim the prize of wholeness and catch a glimpse of who we are in our transparent state. Once we begin to clear our egoic patterns and shadow issues, we find that we are blessed with a heightened sense of discernment, intuition, clarity, transparency, and inner guidance. These arise from having danced at the edge of mystery with our shadows. From succeeding in clearing the way for more Light of Self/Source/Universal Light Energy to shine through; thus, the context behind the true form of the name, *Energy BE-ing.*

Forming the Egoic Self

> *"To change a person must face the dragon of his appetites."*
> —Rumi[19]

Both Leslie Temple Thurston in, *The Marriage of Spirit*[20], and Eckhart Tolle in, *A New Earth*[21] set forth similar ideas around our human personality or ego identification. According to them our personality is a matrix of interlinked energy frequencies forming a design that has shape, structure, density, and finally, an identity that assumes a meaning.

Naming – Toni, John, Pam, Rose, Lance, Bill, Jay, and Sonny – reinforces the sense of the illusion of separation. Then labeling – boy/girl, man/woman, mother/father, and sister/brother – deepens the sense of separation even further.

We then take these ego-identifiers (names and labels) and use them as if they mean something special. "Oh, do you know who *insert name* is?" "Do you know who *insert name* parents are?" "Do you know what *insert name* does for a living?" We further differentiate ourselves with the use of other assigned descriptors such as, anxious/calm, happy/sad, smart/dumb, good/bad, sweet/negative, desirable/undesirable, gay/straight, and so forth.

19 Barks, Coleman (Translator), *The Poetry of Rumi Journal.* Brush Dance. Sausalito, CA.
20 Temple-Thurston, Leslie. *The Marriage of Spirit.* Core Light Publications. Santa Fe, N.M. 2000.
21 Tolle, Eckhart. *A New Earth.* Plume-Penguin Publishing. New York, N.Y. 2005

We then use these descriptors as if they had great meaning. "Did you know *that insert name* is *insert judgment/identifier*?" "He is a bad seed." "My mother, is _____ if you only knew her, then you would know what I am talking about."

Living from this state of confirmed egoic self or human personality tends to corroborate that not only are we separate individuals, but we are alone, living on our own where-with-all. We have locked ourselves into a sense of limitation and have forgotten who we truly are and why we came here to planet earth. Thus, we run around unaware or unconscious of our identity as a 21st century energy being, ONE with a Higher Source and Power.

Why is this Happening to Me- Again?

> *"The Tao doesn't take sides,*
> *it gives birth to both good and evil." [22]*
> --Tao Te Ching

Our true Self/Source is that Essence which lives within us and knows who we truly are in our state of wholeness; without the encumbrance of the "shadow-aspects", without the masks, "conditioned" memories, and delusions of separateness. Connecting with Self opens the way for us to realize that we are sacred humans and allows the *inner witness* to come forth as our guide on the journey back to remembering.

Through connecting with the inner witness – which is a different voice from that of our continuous and negative monkey mind chatter – we have the opportunity to observe the traits within the shadow-side of consciousness from an objective stance. We do this through self-observation. Self-observation is the prelude to greater awareness of self (little me, ego) and Self (Higher Source), for it ultimately leads us into the spiritual, emotional, psychological, and social experiences that we require in order to shed old beliefs.

e.g., Have you ever watched yourself say "no" to something you really wanted and then ask yourself, "Why did I say 'no'?" It was your inner witness that watched the whole process from within your being and then opened the way for you to see what it was that you were doing and why you were doing it. However, you had to consciously say, "yes" to noticing and then being interested in what was being revealed by the inner witness.

The act of making *conscious choices* is imperative to evolution and to soul growth. We must decide what it is we want to express in our lives. If we do not decide, the Universe will decide for us and we probably won't like its decision; for it is its nature to bring us more of what we already have.

---

[22] Lao-Tze. Stephen Mitchell (trans). *Tao Te Ching.* Chapter 5.

What happens when we refuse to make conscious choices? We end up reliving our old patterns repeatedly, all the while crying our same old crocodile tears and lamenting; "Why is this happening to me again?" We are conditioned as children by those around us: our parents, our teachers, our ministers, etc. to be like they are.

This conditioning creates the "conditioned" mind and it lives within our sub-conscious. It provides us with a sense of who and what we are in the world, but it is based on information that has been impressed upon us, not discovered for ourselves – that is why we call it "conditioned" mind – and often it consists of negative information and input.

To the extent we make the choice to continue to identify with the egoic structuring that we were conditioned with is the extent to which we stay stuck in limited and unbalanced patterns. All the while, continuing to ask, "Why is this happening to me again?"

Based upon the beliefs and ideals that have been indoctrinated, we begin to label our experiences as good or bad, happy/sad, naughty/nice, right/wrong, etc. We then make judgments about those experiences based upon our perceptions, which nearly always based on faulty information. We project our perceptions onto the experience, these perceptions were formed in and received from our childhood, which reside in and working through our adult mind.

Ego Identification Loses its Support

"Now" energy is a compassionate energy that desires to move us from outer seeking, to the inner knowing of who we are. Do not be deluded, we will have to continue to remain on high alert in order to remain conscious, but it will take less energy as we peel away the shadows and the masks of illusion and call forth more "Light"/Energy.

As the masks of illusion peel away, we see ourselves more clearly; we see who and what we are at our most authentic level. Because we have been willing to confront our deepest fears and shine the light of self-honesty upon them, we change. This change frees up more energy to use for other areas of growth and we become more transparent.

When negative situations and conditions arise, that in the past would have caused us to shrink away, or move into a stance of defensiveness, or ... we now face them and give them *no* power or energy; for we know what they are – nothingness and illusion. They have no power any longer to take us down, for we have risen above their negative pull into positive power; we have confronted our shadows and seen them for what they are.

We have moved into a mind-set of conscious choices, of being comfortable with living with what *IS*, rather than manipulating circumstances to bring forth what we think is needed and then trying to force its happening. We realize how much energy it takes to push and insist and we are not willing to engage or give that much energy to something that does not yield positive results.

We have clarity around the fact that we live in a resonant -Q- field of energy and that this field provides us with instant "karma". Instant karma means, if we steal something (even energetically through our thoughts); someone is going to steal from us, almost immediately. We are clear about what this instant karma feels like, so we make the conscious choice to live in ease and grace. We consciously cooperate with the energetic Q fields of information that are arising and wanting our attention in order to teach us, instead of pushing our own agendas. Old information about who we thought we were and how we had to support our ego identification collapses and dies.

Energetic vampires and chaos cravers are recognized for who and what they are – people with unskilled behaviors. We find that we are no longer "called" to support these unskilled behaviors; we do not try to change them, we model new behaviors.

We move from fear of not being ___ (enough, worthy, happy, success...) to making a conscious decision or choice for reconnection with Source Energy, our wholeness.

We *BE* the Truth of our <u>BE</u>-ing rather than that which we identify with as what we do, have, want, don't want, see as wrong, fear, worry about, etc. We *BE* that which we want to see in the world and when we are THAT we are free.

> *"The degree to which I seek, another's approval*
> *to that degree am I attached to their disapproval."*
> --Paul Hasselbeck

Making the Unconscious—Conscious and Integrating the Opposites

> *"The more we study reality,*
> *the more we run up against a wall of mysteries."*
> --*What the Bleep Do We Know*, 2004

In the process of self-discovery, we learn to account for the "missing pieces of our lives". We cannot pretend that any part or aspect of our being does not exist – this is part of the movement into authentic being, and of being transparent and whole (whole means that we are in harmony and balance with our self and our energies, it is a unification of energies).

To be whole, to be in balance, we must unify the polarities that exist within us. To unify the polarities requires that we first recognize them, then move though our fears and conditioned beliefs around them. Doing this shifts us and our old beliefs into "higher" states of vibration. This process is referred to as, "making the unconscious – conscious".

e.g., As mentioned earlier as children we were conditioned by the beliefs and values of our authority figures as to what we were to consider as right/wrong, moral/sinful, good/bad, objectionable/non-objectionable, and what constituted the perfect couple, or peaceful or angry actions, etc.

All of these, aforementioned opposites are known as, polarities. Polarities are two poles of opposite or opposing thoughts, one of which we have judged to be good and the other to be not so good or bad. Until we awaken to the limitation that this conditioning places upon us, we continue to make these types of judgments. Judgments based on the conditioning we received from our family and cultural setting, instead of from our own sense of self.

From our conditioned beliefs and subsequent judgments, we learn to embrace or abhor the various aspects of each of these polarities that we experience in life. If we abhor them, we run from them or, use a coping mechanism when in their presence.

e.g. If we were taught or conditioned to believe that anger expressed in any way shape or form was wrong, rather than risk going against our family "values," and daring to express our anger we "stuff" our feelings of anger and try to be calm, good, or play the peace-maker. When we stuff our feelings, overtime we being to pay an energetic price, for after a while stuffing energy begins to deplete us. Here is how it energetically depletes us.

After many episodes of repressing our anger (or whatever it is that we end up trying to repress or hide), we develop a persona (a façade, mask, or guise) around it and this persona (mask) begins to run our lives. The persona takes on a powerful, albeit negative, alternative energetic form.

Hidden deep within the recesses of our subconscious mind the repressed anger feelings, or, whatever it is that we are hiding, begins to operate outside of our conscious awareness and we begin to take on a persona or mask that is socially more acceptable than what was deemed unacceptable by our authority figures.

In order to cope with our non-expressed feelings and beliefs we run to the refrigerator to get something to eat, we develop a sarcastic wit, or we start to indulge in drinking, spending, drugs, sex, and/or other alternative ways of coping. Regardless of what we choose, the bottom line is that instead of responding in a healthy manner, we use an alternative method of expression. One that we perceive is considered more tolerable within the confines of our social structure.

Much of the sense of fragmentation in our lives is caused by the wearing of masks and false personas; masks that are intended to cover up what we have repressed or rejected. However, as we have already seen just because we put on a mask or persona does not mean that our issues go away. We have simply hidden behind them; they still exist within us in the depths of our subconscious mind.

Seeing polarities in the old framework or context of one better than another, causes us to want to reject and suppress the "bad" one, rather than seeing each one as two aspects of wholeness – or our wholeness. Everyone has a shadow-side.

Willingly participating in shadow-work teaches us how to work appropriately with each side of the polarities that exists in us and in the world; as we initiate the process of unifying the opposites this act of unification manifests in our lives as wholeness, balance and transparency.

Our shadow-side is not just about negative conditioning and other "un-wholly" stuff. The shadow, also, contains those glorious aspects of our being that we are afraid of and are not yet ready to fully embrace and accept.

Our fear of these wonder-filled aspects of who we are, along with conditioned feelings of "not enough" or "not acceptable" or ... have caused us to push the aspects out of sight. They remain hidden until we are ready to believe in ourselves. Thus, the sub-conscious contains all that we deny and fear, including the wondrous parts that we do not recognize as of yet, as being the true expression of who we are.

True _Self-discovery begins when we are willing to be interested enough to ask questions such as, "Who am I?" Or, "What is the opposite of the trait I am expressing right now, and how can I express it?"

Being willing to ask these questions takes us into another dimension of our self and can surprise the heck out of us. To create a truly great life, we must reclaim both sides of the polarities that reside within our being and this can only begin when we are willing to be self-aware. Self-awareness is the prelude to awakening to a higher consciousness. One cannot ripen in spiritual maturity without it.

People tend to fear the subconscious mind and project that all of its contents are negative and destructive. This is not true. Saying "yes" to entering the subconscious realm places us on the path of returning – returning and remembering – the knowledge of our oneness and multi-dimensionality. But we must develop a willingness to unveil the contents if we are to return.

Until we willingly enter the mystery of the subconscious (the individual and collective unconscious realm), we will not and cannot discover the vast reservoir of understanding, hidden treasures, pearls of wisdom, and multitude of other skills that we were not aware of having. These and more are the gifts that we have access to once we begin the journey inward.

> *"The art of individualization ... becoming one's unique self ... [is] to discover who we are ... [and] we must ultimately withdraw those parts of ourselves which we have unwittingly projected onto others, thus learning to find deep within our own psyches the potentials and short comings which we had only seen in others."*
> --John Randolph Price
> *The Angels Within Us*

We say, "yes", to participating in shadow-dancing work because we are ready to end our sense of suffering, to stop hiding, and to stop nurturing the illusions that we have been living under. It has been said that we do not change or leave status quo until the pain of staying is greater than the pain of leaving or changing. Thus, we say, "yes" to change because life, through its myriad of experiences, has brought us to a realization that trying to be perfect or something other than that which we truly are, is an illusion that we can never meet and one that has become very costly to our psyche and our soul.

We possess every trait that we encounter in life, bar none, and we possess its opposite. If you believe you are unworthy, seek to find it's opposite, worthiness; it lives in you – seek and you will find it. Once we accept that we are showing up in life as weak, unworthy, over-confident, insecure, etc.; , we can imagine its opposite and start to live that awareness.

We must give our self-permission to experience and feel all facets of who we are; we must be aware of our self as greedy in order to know that we want to be unselfishness. If we are insecure, there resides within us a secure being. We must willingly embrace both aspects of who we are – this includes our power, competence, authenticity, success, beauty, intelligence, and so much more. We learn by contrast. That is the way the universe teaches its lessons.

As we consciously remove our masks and personas, we live from the ground of our being – wholeness. Embrace and integrate all the aspects of being – negative and positive – for through embracing the shadow we learn how to *BE* wholeness in expression.

A "Mystery" Practice: What Shaped My Shadow and My Perceptions?

You will need a journal or several sheets of paper for this experience. On the left hand side of your paper, draw a line about an inch wide, down the side of the paper. At the top of the column you have just created, place the word Age. Now create two more columns down the paper equal distant apart from each other. Place the word Positive at the top of one of these columns and Not so Positive at the top of the other. You have three columns, one "skinny" on the left and two wider ones to the right.

In the Age column, going down the page, create a chronological age list, leaving at least two spaces between each age. Starting with the age 1 then go to 5, 10, 15, 20, 25, 30, 35, 40, 45, 50, and so on, depending upon your current age.

Age	Positive	Not so Positive
1 →5		
5		
10		

Finding a quiet space, where you will not be interrupted, ask yourself the following questions; as the answers arise, make a note at the corresponding age:

- What do I consider the major defining Positive Events/ Experiences of my life?
- List your responses next to the age range in which they occurred.
- What do I consider the major defining Not so Positive or Negative Events/Experiences of my life?
- List your responses next to the age range in which they occurred.
- After you have completed the exercise, review your list.
- Do you see any repeating patterns in either of columns?
- If so, how have they impacted your belief systems and conditioned your actions in life?
- How have they impacted how you show up or reveal yourself to others in life?
- Do you see any thoughts, behaviors, attitudes, or actions that you participate with or in that stem from the conditioning of these experiences?

Age	Positive	Not so Positive
1 →5	I felt loved by mom and dad.	At a play in school, I forgot my lines and the teacher yelled at me, I was embarrassed. My older sister always told me I was stupid and not worthy to live.
5→10	I excelled at school	Mom and Dad divorced
10→ 15	Dad remarried	Mom died My stepmom, yelled at me all the time. I felt unloved and left home.

Repeating Pattern/s or Conditioned Reactions:
Example:
People leave me or I leave them.
How did this pattern impact my thoughts, beliefs, and/or actions?

> I do not let people get close to me. I always hold something back.
> I don't trust easily. When people try to get close, I withdraw.

How do I tend to cope when I find myself in these types of situations? List:

Example:

I tend to sabotage my good

How did this pattern impact my thoughts, beliefs, and/or actions?

> I see that when things go good for me, I do something to assure that I will have to leave or quit.

How do I tend to cope when I find myself in these types of situations?
> List:

Now that you can see these patterns, both positive and not so positive; and the impact each has had on your perceptions, belief systems and actions, you can begin to make conscious choices as to how you will change in order to experience life in a new way.

Commit to doing something that will consciously connect you to the Truth of your Essence. Consciously choose to do this instead of drinking, eating, taking drugs, projecting on others, or whatever coping mechanism you are currently using.

Take one of the repeating patterns or conditioned reactions and create a behavioral goal that will support you in shifting this "old" belief-perception-attitude into a new behavior, attitude, expectation, and action.

When I act/feel/experience/...
I will do/speak/journal/talk to/ ...
> *e.g., when I start to feel the need to withdraw, I will ask myself healthy questions, such as:

"What do I really want to experience in and for my life?"

"To what purpose is my reaction serving as a greater
  Good or contribution for all involved?"

"What do I want to design as my future outcome?"

"What right action can I take that will make this a
  win/win/win situation for all involved?"

"How can I BE clarity in this situation?
 I am not my job, my profession, my title, I am Essence in expression."

*e.g., When I feel abandoned, unworthy, betrayed...
I will ... (write in a journal, take a walk, clear my head with affirmations, seek out a coach, etc.)

*What do you notice?
Do you feel different about your experiences?

What happened to you thru participating in this exercise?

This exercise is meant to open the way for you to experience, notice, and consciously participate in shifting the meanings you have previously given to your experiences and the patterns of behaviors they created and to reconnect to your higher Source, your wholeness, to who you BE – rather than what you do, have, or feel.

Our perceptions create our reality and give meaning to our interpretations of that reality. In other words:

Life has only the meaning we give it!

Life has only the meaning we give it! Think about this!
What experiences have you
given great meaning to in your life;
"She did this – He did that?"
Are you ready to let them go and to
connect to a Higher Truth and way of BE-ing?
--TGB

We are One – Interrelated and Interconnected

"... The greater the tension, the greater the potential.
Great energy springs from a correspondingly
great tension of opposites."[23]
--Carl Jung

Spiritual teachings across the various traditions teach us that our sense of separation from _S_ource and each other is an illusion, a non-reality. Now, quantum physics is confirming this, research is revealing through empirical data, that indeed everything is interrelated at the quantum energetic level (-Q-field). Yet, the illusion we see is that we are separate, and the sense of separation remains, for there are many of us, who are as yet, unconscious to these deeper truths.

The illusion is created through our beliefs and perceptions, which in turn, creates our reality. Perceptions are nothing more than collected patterns of thought-energies or beliefs that gather energetically. They form from our individual and collective experiences, and then become stuck. Thus, we only think that we are separate for we are conditioned to label aspects of our being in order that we can justify our whole belief systems.

In the journey of conscious evolution, we (humankind) are right where we need to be. The "Universe" has gone to a great deal of trouble to develop individual personality as an aspect of humankind – for it is through

---

[23] Jung, Carl; Collected Works 13, Alchemical Studies; Princeton/Bollinger, New York; pg. 118

personality that Spirit takes expression. The lesson we came to learn is the difference between our true Self (capital S-Higher Source) and human personality (small s-self).

We Live in a Holographic Universe

"Like everything else in nature, the life of man is subject to
the law of cause and effect. The present reaps what the past has sown,
and the future is the product of the present." [24]
--Buddha

Quantum physics says the world is a holographic universe where each part contains the pattern of the whole. If this is true and it is, then we contain an aspect of everything that we see and experience, regardless of the judgment we have placed upon it.

This is not said as a condemnation or to elicit shame, guilt, or blame but, rather, to evoke a sense of awareness; for self-awareness is how overcoming begins. When we own that we are responsible for our lives and that everything is interconnected with all that is, then we can begin to shift our perceptions about life and change our world, through the act of being conscious.

As we shape our human personality, our egoic self, our "shadow-stuff" takes shape also, being formed out of the emotional residue of those experiences that life shares with us. Gradually, over time, we repress these negative/toxic emotional aspects of self and bit-by-bit they begin to form beliefs, which become our "shadow-self".

The sub-conscious mind is universally programmed to store all knowledge: all the positive, wonder-filled things that we experience; and all the rejected, unacknowledged, and sociably unacceptable junk that we experience. It then holds all of this stuff for future recall, as needed, in the midst of an experience.

While we are unconscious there is usually an attempt to bury anything that we have learned that has a negative value. Hiding these things from conscious awareness creates a state of denial, which shows up later on down the path of life as an unconscious behavior, belief, attitude, or ways of being. This state of denial happens to us both as individuals and as a collective society.

Each time we deny any aspect of our experiences, those aspects get buried deeper in the sub-conscious or unconscious mind. The unconscious behavior, which is elicited, evolves out of the continued repression of feelings, thoughts, emotions, etc. In the collective society of humankind, this repressed behavior becomes part of what has been labeled as the "collective unconscious".

---

[24] Carus, Paul (comp.). *The Teachings of Buddha.* pg. 30

After a while these repressed beliefs, roles and emotions begin to surface and take form within our personality and our life – whether we are consciously aware of them or not – and most of the time we are not. It is these repressed thoughts that arise from our sub-conscious mind as our shadow-side. They have the capacity to manipulate us into convoluted thinking that results in justification, rationalization, self-deception, and projection-type behavior.

For example; if we were poor as children and we feel we never had enough – food, clothing, love, etc. – that feeling, over time, in order to survive, gets repressed. As an adult, this repressed feeling will reveal itself as behaviors such as being a big-spender or being a miser – both behaviors stem from the same belief of not having enough. Each one is over-compensation for something that the person feels is missing in them.

Once a new concept is introduced into our awareness, one the reveals how it is that we are showing up in life, we have a choice-point moment; we decide if a change in our behaviors or attitudes interests us enough to do something about it. A point of clarification: most people do not even take notice of their behaviors and attitudes because they are still living from a mind-set that is unconscious.

When we are willing to look at what we are doing, willing to notice, willing to observe how it is affecting others and us and then willing to tell the truth about what we see, we start the journey to being conscious. When we are conscious or aware of our actions we can then start to bring our previously "hidden" aspects out into the light and look at them for what they are – nothing but a perception – a belief that can be changed!

Once we honestly look at our attitudes, behaviors, actions, etc. and recognize them for what they are – conditioned illusions, which we have the capacity to change – we can begin to consciously integrate new awareness's into our lives. Albeit, it takes time. It does not happen overnight and it takes willingness on our part to change or shift. Being and staying conscious requires being interested, being interested, being interested, and then noticing what it is we are interested in.

The Spiritual Warrior at Work in Consciousness

"Close both eyes to see with the other eye."
-Rumi [25]

"As the world turns" is a simple metaphor that holds within it the potential for new beginnings. Every 24 hours, the world spin round and we are brought again to the edge of a fresh day and a new dawning, to renewed hope and opportunities for innovative expressions of new awareness's.

Personally, I am grateful for this turning, for the birth of each new day offers me the opportunity to delve deeper into the mystery of the unknown. Doing so affords me the chance to change, to grow, to face new "ah-ha's!", and to leave behind the old "stuff" that is no longer needed.

I like to think that our experiences in life are the fodder of the compost of life. This compost when correctly tended becomes the fertilizer that enhances the growth of the thought-seeds for the next new beginning. We add to the richness and moistness of the compost, every time we consciously chose to engage with that which is energetically arising through our experiences. Thus, our experiences become the fertilizer for the next crop of new ideas and thoughts and our future.

For instance, we pick up a book and feel a vibration move throughout our being. Perhaps we do not fully understand what is happening, however, we make a conscious choice to engage in the mystery of what is taking place; we choose to read the book. We allow the book to be our teacher, for that moment – it must contain some kernel of truth or we would not have resonated with it. So through our choice we connect with the energy of the moment that is arising and desiring to be noticed. Usually, we do this unconsciously, unaware of what it truly arising or happening – we take it for granted.

As we read, we consciously assimilate the words of the text and the deeper meanings that desire to arise. The residue of richness that evolves from having participated in a conscious moment is the fodder that feeds our soul; and leaves us craving to do it again. The Mystery, unbeknownst to us, is continually drawing us unto Itself and inviting us to sup at its table.

Before I go any further with the story that is about to unfold, for clarity's sake, there is something that I would like to share about myself. I am not a guru chaser! Nor am I a lecture lizard! Neither am I a workshop junkie; I am clear that at this juncture of the journey – my one and only teacher is the inner witness, often called the Holy Spirit. However, occasionally it becomes apparent that there is an "outer" teacher to engage with, in order to deeper till the soil of consciousness.

---

[25]
Barks, Coleman. *The Poetry of Rumi Journal*. Brush Dance Publications. Sausalito, CA.

Hawkins, David M.D. *Power vs. Force*. Veritas Publishing. Sedona, AZ.

Deciding to take the chance to dig deeper into the fecund farmland of the mystery of life, in almost a split-second decision, I chose to pack my bags and go to Sedona, Arizona to attend a lecture. The book that evoked this response, to pick up and go to Sedona, had been hand-carried to me. The person I was going to Sedona to see was author and lecturer, David Hawkins M.D. Hawkins is the author of multiple best-selling books including, "*Power vs. Force* [26]", and "*The Eye of the I*". [27],

Hawkins is an engaging, humorous, eccentric, earthy, spiritual, and intelligent being; and all of these afore mentioned characteristics live in a wiry, small-framed package that has survived more than seven decades and several en'lighten'ment -type experiences.

Allow me to regress for a moment as I set the stage for the Saturday lecture experience. Prior to arriving in Sedona, I had made an appointment to meet Hawkins, on the Friday before the lecture. The meeting was a private session held at his home. The experience, for me, was an interesting composite of gaiety, informality, and self-observation; seasoned with a large helping of clarity.

After our time together, as I was exiting the Hawkins home, another guest stopped me and shared that I might want to get to the retreat center early the next morning, as the seats upfront fill quickly. The next thing that happened was one of those moments that make you sit up and take notice.

Almost in the same instant that the person uttered the advice, my Inner Witness, Holy Spirit shared; "If there is only truth being expressed in that room and I am one with It, it does not matter where one sits." "Yes," I said to myself, consciousness would do what it needs to do, to me and through me, regardless of my placement.

The clarity of the truth of this declaration resounded throughout my being and somewhat shocked me, as if being whacked with an electric cattle prod. I realized I was not to make a comment. I knew this message and moment were for my "ears" only. My work was to take note of it and allow it to be fodder for the compost. So I simply smiled at the person, said "Thank you", and made my exit.

The next morning I arrived at the retreat center and found that the person had been correct. People were lined up to get a front row seat. Remembering what Spirit had placed upon my heart the day before, I consciously chose not to engage in the stampede for a "good" seat and selected a chair in the very last row.

As I listened to Hawkins share the various truths and wisdoms that the spiritual experiences of life had graced him with, one that caught my attention

---
[26] Hawkins, David M.D. *Power vs. Force.* Veritas Publishing. Sedona, AZ.
[27] Ibid

was an idea regarding, movements in consciousness. He described these movements as a *"Map of the Scale of Consciousness"*.

According to Hawkins movements on the scale of consciousness map occur when a person rises from one level of awareness to another on the scale; and Hawkins has mathematically calibrated the scale.

What peaked my interest, that morning, was a discussion on the movement from the level of pride to courage and onto love. The levels of awareness on the map are not set-up in a hierarchical fashion, per se. However, Hawkins says that the movement from one level to the next enfolds the awareness of the previous level into the next. Thus, the map of consciousness is a descriptive listing of the upper, progressive unfolding of conscious awareness. (The "map of the scale consciousness"[28] is in the book, Power *vs. Force*.)

I closed my eyes and engaged in the practice of conscious, intentional "interior listening" as Dr. Hawkins spoke. Listening with my attention focused in my heart is a practice originally taught by the ancient desert fathers; and, more recently, scientifically proven to be of great value by Doc Lew Childres, founder of Heart-Math.

This silent act of intentional "interior listening", creates a sense of interior spaciousness which "opens" me to engage more consciously with the person to whom I am directing my attention. Intentional interior listening moves me to a level of awareness, which circumvents the words and goes to the "heart" of the energy of the message. It allows me to engage with the deeper essence of the message rather than with the messenger.

So with my ears, I heard Hawkins voice sharing the following: (This is a paraphrase of what I thought I heard him say.)

"Marines enlist people on the level of pride, thus the logo, "Be a Marine". But in order to engage in battle or warfare, one NEEDS more than pride -- one has to move to the next level of awareness, courage."

"It is pride that engages us to join in the cause, whatever that cause may be, but it is courage that allows us to do the things that need to be done once engaged in the cause. Thus, through pride we move the interior warrior into a 'higher' level of consciousness on the map (a new matrix of information or paradigm shift) to that of courage."

"Each new level of information and information opening about self creates a movement on the map. We move along the map, in an upward, progressive, movement of consciousness, until at a certain point the "interior" warrior is transformed by love into the <u>spiritual</u> warrior. The warrior is tempered by the knowledge of Divine Love and becomes the spiritual warrior."

---

[28] Hawkins, David M.D. *Eye of the I* and *Power vs. Force.* Veritas Publishing. Sedona, AZ. pg. Appendix B

Why is it imperative for us to evolve into the spiritual warrior? Part of the answer lies in the words peace and death. Peace is relatively simple, we cannot experience peace on earth until the interior warrior, who is always fighting some cause, knows, and understands life through the eyes of divine Love.

Then the warrior stops fighting everything and everyone, and settles into a deep understanding that – "peace begins with me". Until this happens, in both individual and collective consciousness, acts of war and hate – internal and external – will remain.

As we consciously choose peace, each of us adds to the consciousness of peace until that awareness reaches a critical mass. Critical mass is reached when a greater understanding of unconditional love is realized and made real in our lives; there by, allowing peace to be anchored in conscious awareness.

We do not know what that critical mass number is; however, the conjecture is that it is a relatively small number of the whole of the world population; perhaps, as few as, 1%, 3%, or 5%, of the total population.

Hawkins says that we also need the spiritual warrior in that moment, when we reach the end; when we cross over the threshold of what appears as death. Our spiritual warrior knows and understands Love, and thus, has the capacity to take us across the threshold.

The spiritual warrior's grace is that it allows us to face, the greatest enemy - death; in whatever form it chooses to take – the appearance of dying or of dying to the ego. The spiritual warrior has the healthy and wise combination of pride, courage, and understanding of love of self and Self that is needed to walk through the "illusion" of this world, to the other side.

After all, death is only a movement in consciousness to a new level of awareness. Hawkins also says that, "One cannot reach Enlightenment or Nirvana, without facing the "death and annihilation of the ego".

What I heard Hawkins share, I heard through the art of interior listening, listening with my heart. When Hawkins made his comment on the spiritual warrior's role in enlightenment, in an instant – and when Spirit is at work everything happens in a nano-second – I was embraced by a Light.

Perhaps this is the same Light Saul experienced on the road to Damascus, I do not know. What I do know is that my Light experience was life transforming for hidden within the interior brilliance of that Light was a revelation.

I "saw" before me, all the various ways I had engaged my interior warrior over multiples of lifetimes. Before I could blink, the entire history of my warrior-type "past lives" was shown to me upon the screen of my soul. In many screens, I was a Samurai, dressed in the outfit of the time, in brilliant red silk with gold trim; and in others, I was a religious zealot, a hired warrior, a trained ... I 'saw' them all.

This explosion of awareness did not necessarily happen in a visual experience, it was more like a feeling experience; yet, there were pictures, of a sort. Regardless, it contained a window of opportunity for the possibility of the NOW and PAST to collide.

Undulating, spiraling, waxing and waning, one chasing another; "feeling" pictures sped by. Each picture clamored for my attention. I vacillated between feelings of surprise, remorse, sadness, righteous indignation, and finally, quiet contentment for what 'was' and now IS.

At the end of this multi-lifetime picture show, I was catapulted to the plane above the corn field in Pennsylvania, on 9/11. There, I stood face-to-face with those "warriors". Through silent communication, words without words, Source invited me to view the picture without any judgments; to rise above the content of the feeling images facing me. I was invited, in that moment, to release the "how horrible!" and "how could they?" and move into the context of a "bigger" spiritual picture.

In the same instant as I heard this request, my heart melted and I began to cry. I realized that those men – just as I had done in many of my own life times that I just reviewed – were playing out a movement in consciousness on the Map of the Scale of Consciousness.

It was overwhelming; there are no words to describe the context of that moment. It was so big and so humbling at the same time. And then I heard these words said in a loud and booming voice; "Father, forgive them for they know not what they do!" I was speaking these words silently, interiorly!

I realized that I was being asked to engage in an act of forgiveness greater than anything I had ever imagined or experienced before. I was being asked to move into the consciousness of unconditional love and in this consciousness, send forth love, regardless of the act.

I was asked to *BE* a moment of blessing for the universe; called to forgive, not from the sense of forgiving the acts, but forgiving the unskilled behaviors of those persons I labeled "terrorists". To *BE* a transparency that divine, unconditioned Love could flow forth from and touch the world for one brief second through. It felt cosmic in nature.

And maybe, just maybe, in that moment, I felt, that somewhere in the universe there was someone experiencing something that was overwhelming; and the flow of Love that was being moved through me, was reaching out and touching their conscious awareness.

At the quantum level, we are interconnected and I know that flow of Love could vibrate across a string of energy and touch a heart. Maybe, one person would know for a brief moment that they were not alone, that they were love and that they were loved. I don't know, I do not have any answers, I only have questions, and I can only report what I felt and experienced.

As a transparency for Love, in that moment I was clear that regardless of what we have done while in a body, we are all just souls journeying through the morass of life; and we deserve to be embraced by love. In this human life experience comes a myriad of choices that we are called to make – and each choice is made in the name of soul growth or, not.

The choices only appear to be connected to the content contained within time and space – when perhaps, they are not. Perhaps, all of our choices and subsequent actions are connected to a greater scheme or play of which we have no understanding.

As I felt the unconditioned Love energy begin to flow through my body, a soul wrenching, uncontrollable sob made its way up through my being and out of my mouth. The cry came forth like a spark that sets fire to a field of dry chaff and, once having gained control, there is no stopping it until it has completed its deed.

I couldn't stop the sobbing even if I wanted to, I knew I couldn't. The tears were a healing balm for my soul and for collective consciousness. My spiritual warrior was here and I was being asked to rise above the pride of being embarrassed, of being seen as out of control, as losing it, and allow myself this moment. I wanted to participate fully in the exploration of the mystery at hand and of the Energy desiring to be made known through me.

As the intensity of the cry began to rise, so did the accompanying feeling of unconditioned Love. Love swept over my soul, as a wind that sweeps in and clears all the dust and leaves that remain on the porch after Autumn trees release their goods.

I realized that for each person I was willing to embrace in the arms of unconditioned Love, in the context of the big picture of life and evolution – regardless of whether I knew them or not – I, too, was being forgiven for all the acts of perpetration that I had committed, in this lifetime and others.

As I forgave, as I gave-forth, I was being forgiven. We are all interrelated and interconnected, so perhaps, this is how it has to energetically work.

As I was being given to, from the unconditioned Love of the universe, I was giving forth of the Love being poured through me as a vessel. Love came to me in order to move through and create a movement into a new level of awareness about Love.

To add another dimension to the experience, I noted that as I sat there crying, I was actually outside of myself observing the whole experience. From a physical sense, Hawkins was in the front lecturing, I was in the back crying, and from the context of _Source, I was observing it all.

As _Source was speaking through Hawkins, in that same moment I was being touched by the hand of _Source. This vessel was the one that everything was happening through and as the same time "I" was the watcher of it all. So there you have it, a paradox; for as the world turned in time and space, I was in the midst of a no-time experience.

Oh, there is something else! If you have ever wondered if _Source_ has a sense of humor; when I finally settled down, stopped sobbing, and began to breathe again, my friend whom I went to the lecture with turned to me and said;

"Wow, I do not know what was going on with you, but as you began to cry I turned to look at you and instead of seeing you sitting there – I saw a vision of you as a Samurai- an ancient Oriental warrior!"

The Art of Interior and Generous Listening

"Stop the words now.
Open the window in the center of your chest,
and let spirit fly in and out."
--Rumi [29]

"Interior and Generous Listening" or taking a "Presence Pause"[30] is an opportunity to stop, take a deep breath, and look at what wants to energetically arise, in the moment. Taking a moment to stop and consciously engage in "interior and/or generous listening" gives us the opportunity to choose to be present to the energy of the moment, or not.

It allows us to be interested in shifting awareness from content [the stuff happening] to the greater context [the energy that desires to teach and/or be recognized] and also, to be fully present to the person and/or energy at hand. Whether we are in a situation which is upsetting or calm in a prayer time – we *BE* present to the "needs and desires" of the energy arising.

The intention of interior listening as a practice is to open and awaken us to new levels of awareness and understanding. We are open to the Presence and the present moment; letting them be a catalyst for possibility; the possibility of an extraordinary transforming experience, for self and others, through being generous of spirit, heart, and being.

The concept of interior and generous listening is not new, over 2,000 years ago, the ancient desert fathers consciously focused or centered their attention in the heart space in all they did. This type of practice began with a prayer that was called, *"The Jesus Prayer"*.

The ancient desert fathers, by keeping their attention focused in the heart; learned to pray without ceasing. Staying focused on a Higher Source, their only intention was that of knowing and experiencing that Higher Source. Through interior listening, they experienced spiritual liberation.

"The Philokalia", [31] is a compilation of stories gathered by two Greek Monks in the early 18th century. The stories are about saints, sages, and mystics who, through the act of consciously holding their attention in their heart, ascended into enlightenment. It is said that all traditions have an interior listening-type prayer.

---

[29] Barks, Coleman. *The Poetry of Rumi Journal.* Brush Dance Publications. Sausalito, CA.

[30] Boehm, Toni G. *The Spiritual Intrapreneur.* 1st → 5th printing Dorrance Publishing. Pittsburgh, PA. 1996. Revised printing Inner Visioning Press. Greenwood, MO. 2001. pg. 9

[31] Kadloubovsky, E. and Palmer G. Translators. *The Philokalia.*

In the beginning, many, many years ago, when I started the practice; I struggled with keeping my attention focused in the heart. I had to stay conscious in order to be with the practice. What happens now is that in the midst of difficult situations and peaceful ones, energy arises and invites me to come to the heart; to BE the space of interior listening.

In everyday situations, in conditions of chaos, in meetings where it feels like power struggles might be brewing, in times where one wants it done this way and someone else wants it done that way and this person doesn't think it's being done right at all – I stop, look, and be interested in what the energy is inviting me to notice – and to *BE* present to what that more might be.

Bringing the attention to the heart is a powerful practice. Charles Fillmore, co-founder of Unity states of the heart, in his book *Revealing Word*[32], the heart is:

"...the faculty through which we receive love from Being. The heart is the visible expression of an invisible center of consciousness... It is the invisible center of consciousness through which divine substance is poured forth. Substance is the divine energy that underlies all manifestation, anything that comes into manifestation comes into it through a divine energy. When the heart is purged of thoughts adverse to good then we consciously contact the underlying God substance."

In scripture, the heart represents the subconscious mind. If we have been filling the subconscious with false beliefs, error thoughts and negative impressions, what happens when we bring our attention (our head or mind) down into the heart and consciously focus on interior listening in that space of wisdom? A purification process begins that stokes the fires of transformation – quantum transformation – and a clean-up process in the subconscious mind is activated.

A "Mystery" Practice: The Interior, Generous Listening Meditation

I invite you to get comfortable, let the chair hold your weight as you allow your hands to rest comfortably on your thighs, with your palms extended. We hold as our purpose of this meditation, that we are placing ourselves into relationship with <u>S</u>ource; to experience the spaciousness of emptiness, the expansiveness of <u>S</u>ource Energy.

Take a deep cleansing breath, then focus your attention in the heart space on the breath. Be aware as it rises and then falls back into the heart space. Continue to notice and be interested in the movement of the breath.

32 Fillmore, Charles. *The Revealing Word.* Unity House Publishing. Unity Village, MO. 1959.

Notice how the breath seems to swing in an arc, as you breath in then breath out. At a point, the arc falls back into the heart space; hold your attention on that point; it is that pause, which is the opening to the space between the breaths. It is the still-point, that when we fall through its crack, through its opening, we enter into the spacious of emptiness; the place of connection to Source and Source Energy.

Hold your attention there without any thought other than being present to the point where the breath enters. Allow the breath to arise and fall naturally, you do not have to breath; you are now being breathed. The energy contained within the spaciousness begins to wrap you in its mantle and bless you with its gifts; one of which is love. You are settling deeper into love.

Linger in the heart-space, in the spaciousness, holding the attention in the heart and be present to the energy, notice the pulsing of stillness. This is the act of interior listening. If a thought arises, tries to intrude, or wants to capture your attention – and it will – gently bring the attention back into the heart.

Stay intentional about where your attention is focused; intentionality holds your attention, and attention creates the direction where the mind flows. Your attention is in the spaciousness of the heart. There is a silent rhythm in the heart space, be in alignment with the rhythm of Silence; the Spaciousness of Emptiness.

Take a few moments and be in the energy.

As you, prepare to go forth and live your life, attending to the mundane activities of daily living, continue to consciously practice keeping your attention focused in the heart space. As you gently begin to open your eyes, – use soft eyes – open them ever so slightly while consciously keeping your attention focused in your heart. Look around and notice what you see, while keeping your attention focused in the heart.

Notice what that feels like – to look with soft eyes. How does it feel different from being in a hurry to do the next thing that is showing up? Know that you can look at other people or do other things and remain centered with the attention in the heart. Connecting consciously with the energy of the heart will make a difference in your day and in your life. Prepare for quantum transformations!

"I am now in the presence of Pure Being and immersed in the Holy Spirit of Life, Love and Wisdom. I acknowledge Thy Presence and Thy Power, Oh, blessed Spirit. In Thy Divine Wisdom now erase my mortal limitations and from Thy pure Substance of Love bring into manifestation my world according to Thy perfect Law."
--Charles Fillmore
Holy Spirit Invocation

Chapter 4
BE! A Marriage of Science and Spirituality

"The disciples asked him [Jesus],
why do you teach us in parables?
And answering he said to them,
Because it has been given to you
to know the mysteries...
--Matthew 13:10-11

Science and Spirituality

"If some say to you, 'Where have you come from?'
say to them, 'We have come from the light,
where the light came into being by itself,
established itself, and appeared in an image of light.'[33]
–The Nag Hammadi Library

We are moving from a mindset steeped in Newtonian perspectives – remember, Isaac Newton and the apple tree, which birthed the concept of gravity – into a knowledge that supports and reveals an understanding of the world at the quantum level – the level of the smallest discrete quantity of a physical property.

Quantum research delves into not only the measuring of the smallest unit of a physical property, but also what happens with its energy as the unit moves about. This study of energy at the quantum level is known as, quantum physics. At this point in human development, quantum research is a study of possibilities and probabilities.

Studies substantiating the impact of the discoveries of quantum physics on humankind can now be found in writings such as *The Field* and *The Intention Experiment* [34], *Quantum Leaps* [35], *The Hidden Parables*[36], *The Biology of Belief* [37], and many other books. These works are sharing information, in a form that is easily readable by those not steeped in the principles and mathematics of quantum physics.

What these authors and others, including myself, are providing for their readers, are understandable approaches to the mysteries being uncovered and how these _Q_ mysteries relate to the unchanging principles of spirituality (the quality of being spiritual, living principle). How these principles work with us, when we are willing, and how they can shift our consciousness and transform our lives. Through research, study, and self-inquiry researchers,

[33] Meyer, Marvin W. (trans.). *The Secret Teachings of Jesus: Four Gnostic Gospels.* pg.28
[34] McTaggert, Lynne M. *The Field and The Intention Experiment.* Free Press. New York, N.Y. 2005 and 2007
[35] Shelton, Charlotte. *Quantum Leaps.* Butterworth-Heinemann. Boston, MA. 1999.
[36] Todd, Michael. *The Hidden Parables.* Jeremy P. Tarcher/Penquin. New York, N.Y. 2006
[37] Lipton, Bruce. *The Biology of Belief.* Mountain of Love/Elite Books. Santa Rosa, CA. 2005. reference only

including myself, are discovering correlations between quantum concepts and spiritual principles and that a "marriage" of the two has the capacity to create quantum growth in conscious awareness.

In the following chart, quantum scientific concepts and spiritual principles are partnered based on similar intent. Reflect upon the quantum concept and then its partner, the spiritual principle; as you do this be interested in your personal responses and notice what comes to your awareness from being open.

Please take note, as you work with this chart, it is not meant to be an end all, be all, definition and partnering of these two ideas. It is a first attempt at joining these two concepts and allowing them to *BE* in relationship, as they dance at the edge of mystery – together.

> *"...the microscopic landscape is suffused with tiny strings*
> *whose vibrational patterns orchestrate*
> *the evolution of the cosmos."* [38]
> --Brian Greene, Ph.D.

A Marriage of (-Q-) Quantum Concepts and Spiritual Principles

-Q- Concepts and Spiritual Principles

Quantum Concept-Theory	*Spiritual Truths and Principles*
-Q- Concept: *Theory of Energy*	*Spiritual Truth or Principle:* *Thoughts are Things*
It is energy, not matter, which is the primary substance and building block of the universe.	Thoughts are energy in potential. Whether our thoughts are gathered into belief systems, set as intentions, spoken or acted upon – it is all energy – so be conscious of what you think, feel, speak, and do. Affirmation: I am a power-filled creator! Spiritual Truth or Principle: There are no accidents We are made in the image and likeness of God. There is only One

[38] Greene, Brian. *The Elegant Universe: Superstrings, Hidden Dimensions and the Quest for the Ultimate Theory.* W.W. Norton and Co. N.Y. N.Y. pg. 135.

-Q- Concept:
Quantum Participation and
Quantum Potential

Spiritual Truth or Principle:
All Is One

The quantum realm is participatory and it possesses an infinitely sensitive feedback system that is connected to the whole of everything.

These concepts also reveal that the universe is a field of energetic information that acts as a hologram. Each of us is a web or network of energy fields; there are both individual and collective memory fields contained in this invisible realm. These fields vibrate messages and can be picked up by those who have "ears" to hear.

This Q field is a source of tremendous potential that we can tap into and it has immense energy; if harnessed, the energy in one cell can blow up a six-story building.

The universe is a field of invisible, interconnected energy networks, which are always broadcasting and creating synchronistic opportunities. The more aligned with the field we are; the more synchronicities (or, synchro-divinities) occur in our life. Make a change in one area of life and the change will be reflected in all areas of our life.

Affirmation:
I am a mighty attractor for Good!

-Q- Concept:
Unified Field Theory

Spiritual Truth or Principle:
Truth is Simple

Underneath the physical world's appearance of diversity there is a basic simplicity.

Truth is simple and the Law works if you work it!

Affirmation:
I am creative by design!

-Q- Concept:
Theory of Everything

Spiritual Truth or Principle:
Law of One

There is a fundamental unifying principle that ties all

There is only One Presence and One Power and it is Truth.

forms back together in a simple way.

We are speaking of the Absolute Truth, with a capital T.
The Truth IS and IS always IS-ing

Affirmation:
My "Yes" goes forth and will not return empty for my words have the power of the Divine Idea that animates them.

-Q- Concept:
Theory of Attraction

Spiritual Truth or Principle:
Law of Attraction

A particle's charge will influence how it will respond to other particles. Positive and negative charges create electrical fields, which in turn, create magnetic fields, and magnetic fields are an attractor – like a magnet and iron filings.

What I put out as an energetic thought returns back to me. Neutral neither attracts nor repels – think about this!
Affirmation:
I am clear and clarity of intention attracts back to me in like fashion.

-Q- Concept:
Theory of Self-
Organization

Spiritual Truth or Principle:
God-Spirit-Higher Power-
Intelligence – Light –
Energy ... IS and is in
everything; rocks, trees,
people, animals...
Involution Proceeds Evolution

The universe is a hologram and inherent within each atom/quanta of the universe is intelligence, a self-organizing code that is continually evolving the universe – it is like a DNA code. As with a hologram, each part is infused with the implicate order of the whole.
Each of the foundational quantum waves that make up the universe are akin to the DNA (genetic information) in

A Higher Intelligence permeates everything, this Intelligence knows how to evolve Itself and create Order out of chaos.
(Additionally, ancient masters taught and modern day spiritual teachers continue to teach the principle that God is everywhere present, all knowing, and all powerful; a.k.a., Omnipresent, Omniscient, and Omnipotent)
Involution precedes evolution. Involution according to the dictionary means: involving, entangling, or folding

humans; inherent in each wave is universal information that can replicate the universe. All the knowledge and wisdom of the universe is contained in each quantum wave, it is a microcosm of the macrocosm.

in upon itself.

Involution is a part of the process of the intelligent evolution of thought.

Information from Divine Mind or "above" must come "down" into the realm of the physical to be utilized. If it is worked with consciously we evolve to higher levels of awareness and en'lighten'ment in consciousness.

Affirmation:
I am perfect order and intelligence in expression!

-Q- Concept:
Chaos Theory

Inherent in order is the element of chaos.

In Genesis 1 (*Holy Bible;* Hebrew Testament) the Holy Spirit brooded over the chaotic energy of Creation/ Substance; after a time, it gathered and reflected Itself as Light – Energy.

Spiritual Truth or Principle:
Change is Fundamental to
Transformation

In order for anything to shift, change, or transform it must undergo a shift of some sorts, like water to ice. In the midst of the transformation experience no energy is lost, it is only transformed into something different; and so it is with us when we undergo change in our lives.

Rupert Sheldrake purports that for change to occur on the human level it happens two ways:

1. Through the creation of intention.
2. Through critical mass.

Example: Critical mass: in the 1980s, did people even consider having a personal computer, let alone a laptop? No, it did not live in consciousness as a collective possibility. Now, how could we live without them? We reached a critical mass in consciousness and now computers are a part of the human paradigm. They are common to everyday life; we do not give them a second thought.

Affirmation:
I welcome change as I would
Friend!

-Q- Concept:
Theory of Interconnection

At the quantum level
everything is in relationship.
Relationships are the foundation
of everything for all is
interconnected and interrelated
–and boundaries are shared.

-Q- Concept:
The Observer Effect

The human mind influences
its environment and affects the
way that matter and energy
interact at the subatomic level[39]
. The observer has the power to
alter what is being observed.

The double-slit experiment
was conducted to reveal the
nature of photons, bundles of
light energy. The research
queried, were these bundles,
particles or waves? The
revelation was that when the
photons are unobserved they act
as a wave (infinite possibility).
When observed, the wave
collapsed into a particle (form-
making).

Meaning that as long as the
photon is unobserved, it is a
wave of infinite possibility and
potential. The consciousness of
the observer collapses the wave
into a form or expression,

Spiritual Truth or Principle:
Law of One

What I do to you, I do to me!
Therefore, I do unto others as I would
have them do unto me, *The Golden Rule.*

Affirmation:
I am *That*!

Spiritual Truth or Principle:
Law of Mind Action
Principle of Expansion

Law of Mind Action – We live in a
universe of infinite possibility, with the
capacity to create through our thoughts.
Thoughts held in mind produce in the
outer after their kind. What I hold as a
constant thought-energy gathers more
energy and becomes a belief and my
beliefs are reflected in my life through
my experiences.

Thoughts are energy and when they
collect or gather, they form a belief
system. Our perceptions of our
experiences, what we observe in life,
influence our thoughts. Like thoughts
gather or clump together and create
beliefs. Perceptions influence our beliefs
and our beliefs create our experiences,
which influence our perceptions. It is a
vicious circle and it can be changed.

In the "delayed choice experiment"[41],
beams of photons were sent from one end
of a lab to the other, through two paths
(P-A and P-B). The photon/light always

---

[39] Todd, Michael. *The Hidden Parables.* Jeremy P. Tarcher/Penguin. New York, N.Y. 2006. pg.
[41] Wheeler, John. 1922 Nobel Peace Prize.Princeton.

according to their intention.

We live in a universe of infinite possibility (energetic waves) which we, have the capacity to turn into particles (form) and create our reality out of, in accordance with our intentions and conscious awareness. We observe life, assign meaning (judge) to what we observe, then defend what we have created from our judgments and observations. *"When you enter particle reality, you have collapsed the wave of infinite potentials into a world of opposites: light/dark, good/bad, right/wrong, on/off...only one choice can exist at a time in the particle reality...[when you feel] judgmental, defensive, aggressive, etc. in an effort to manage your discomfort...step back...allow for all possibilities to exist."* [40]

Create a new reality!

chose the path being observed. If the observer moved from P-A to P-B, so did the light – AND – it erased all of its history of having been on P-A. It changed its past history! Think about this!

-Q- Concept:
Tunneling

Spiritual Truth or Principle:
Challenges and Conflict are
Opportunities for (Soul) Growth

Sub-atomic particles can tunnel through energy barriers. If two sub-atomic particles leave the gate at the same time and speed, and one encounters an obstacle on the path and the other doesn't, the particle that encountered the obstacle will

Think about how this equates to the problems we encounter in our lives, i.e., when we are open to seeing the good in a difficult situation don't we learn and grow from having experienced the situation? Even if the lesson we learn is that we do not want to experience that again!

In addition, this refers to the

40
Simmons, Gary and Bonario, Rima. *The Art and Practice of Living w/ Nothing and No One Against Me.* The -Q- Effect. pg. 117.

arrive at the finish line before the one who didn't.

underlying message of Albert Einstein's statement: "You cannot solve a problem on the same level that created it."

Affirmation:
"I look, see, tell the truth, and take authentic action."

-Q- Concept:
Theory of Relativity

The foundation of the universe is: $e=mc^2$. Energy is the foundation of the universe. Energy is a law, it never changes; thus, through the law of mathematics we can calculate not only speeds of light, but our check book balance.

Spiritual Truth or Principle:
Law of Creation

The foundational element of everything in the universe is energy and Light (along with unconditioned love) is the highest form of that energy.

In all major spiritual traditions, God is referred to as Light and is said to have created through the Power of Light and Love.

Universal laws are not haphazard, they are dependable and immutable, and they always work. A universal law is a principle of creation that operates in all phases of life and existence, everywhere, all the time.

Affirmation:
Universal Good (the "YES!" pulse of the universe) is always working to give me my highest and best Good!

-Q- Concept:
Speed of Light [42]

The speed of light is 186,350 miles per second. It is a constant, it never changes, and it is the fastest form of energy. *Light*, therefore, *is the most*

Spiritual Truth or Principle:
Law, Principle, Spirit, Source, God, Light, and Energy

Law, Principle, Spirit, Source, God, Light, and Energy are the same and never change. Principle is the same today, as it was yesterday, and will be

---

[42] Trevithick, Grant. *The Cosmic Puzzle.* Quantum Spirituality Press. Chester, N.J. 2005. pgs. 25-33

powerful form of energy in the universe.

-Q- Concept:
Duality/Polarity [43]

If two sub-nuclear particles are separated and one is spun in one direction, say clockwise; the other will automatically begin to spin in the opposite direction on its own.

tomorrow. If it is of Source, it can never change.

Affirmation:
I am Energy in expression!
I am the Light of the world
and I let my Light shine!

Spiritual Truth or Principle:
Danger/Peace; the Two are
One

In the Chinese language the same character that is used for the word "peace", is also used for the word "danger". They are considered two sides of one coin.

To know peace, one must first know danger – otherwise how would they know when they are experiencing peace?

Life and the experiences of life are only understood through contrast and through reflection upon the contrasts – light/dark, up/down, male/female, good/evil...

Experiences are understood only through contrast and reflection.

How would we know what is good, if we didn't experience something not so good?

By taking the time to reflect upon what happened within an experience, we learn. What we learn is that conscious, intentional choices determine the outcome of situations.

Opposites are two sides of one coin, they work together as one energy force to teach us by contrast.

Affirmation:
I am intentional and conscious in my choices!

---

[43] Trevithick, Grant. *The Cosmic Puzzle.* Quantum Spirituality Press. Chester, N.J. 2005. pg. 41

-Q- Concept:
String Theory [44]

Spiritual Truth or Principle:
We are all – One
The Law of Cause and Effect
Our Words have Power

The fundamental element of the universe is strings of energy. This energy is composed of one-dimensional, vibrating strings that are identical until the frequency of their vibration changes.

These strings contain, like DNA, all the knowledge, and wisdom of the universe and because of this, we have the ability to affect not only our present moment, but our future and past also; through the power of our thoughts.

This concept was proven by John Wheeler, 1922 Nobel Prize Winner through his "Delayed Choice Experiments".

The DCE revealed that not only did the observer affect the movement of photon/light but the photon changed its past history in order to appear in alignment with the observer.

Déjà vu` is thought to occur through string energy containing past, present, and future knowledge. In some manner, usually through sleep, future information "leaks" from these strings of energy and then at some future moment we "catch" up with it and remember we had previously dreamt about this moment. Everything is in

Ancient texts proclaim, "I am you, you are me, and we are one".

Thus, what you do affects and has an effect on me because it's all energy and the energy of what you put into the universe be it fear or love, gathers with other energies of a similar nature and creates belief systems that live in the collective psyche. This race consciousness impinges and affects all of us.

What I send forth is thought-energy, positive or negative, and what will return to me is energy; although it may be in another form, it will be vibrating at the same frequency as what I sent forth.

My words, made up of thoughts are imbued with energy and I send them forth each time I speak; and that energy will not return to me empty.

Energy is never destroyed it just changes shape!

Affirmation:
My words have power and return to me with the same energy frequency as which they were sent forth!

[44] Trevithick, Grant. *The Cosmic Puzzle.* Quantum Spirituality Press. Chester, N.J. 2005. pg. 50.

relationship and interconnected at the quantum level.

-Q- Concept:
Non-Locality [45]

Particles transmit information instantaneously between themselves, even when separated by miles.

Spiritual Truth or Principle:
Law of Attraction
Like Attracts Like

There is an old adage, which says, "Once in relationship, always in relationship". If someone touches our life, they will always be a part of our life and live in our heart regardless of where they are in the world.

Additionally, when we are in resonance with a person or condition we will draw that person or condition to us. Synchronicity, is nothing more than resonant fields colliding, at the right time and place.

Every cell of our being has substance, life, and intelligence; it has the energy of the universe within it. Our cells have the intelligence of the universe within them and have the capacity through that intelligence to tap into the life force and call it forth at greater and greater depths of awareness.

Affirmation:
I am a radiating center of Divine Love, a channel of healing energy. I know what to do and I do it!

-Q- Concept: Quantum
Leaps and Parallel Universes
Multi--Dimensions

The smallest movement at the sub-atomic quantum level, which is invisible to the naked eye, has the capacity to create

Spiritual Truth or Principle:
Life is Consciousness

As we consciously work with the principles, a shift in consciousness occurs or happens. This shift may take a

---

[45] Trevithick, Grant. *The Cosmic Puzzle.* Quantum Spirituality Press. Chester, N.J. 2005. pg. 51.

major shifts in its environment.

There are scientists who believe that we are simultaneously living in multi-dimensions or parallel universes. Their theories are that when we make a major life decision, that decision is played out across multiple or parallel universes and that we can have access to the answers of "What would have happened if..?"

As one might expect this is not a theory espoused by many.

period of time or it may happen in the blink of an eye.

The smallest shift in awareness can change our lives significantly, for we have opened the way for more light-energy to flow into conscious awareness. New matrices of information are available for "downloading".

Universal truths that support this Life is Consciousness principle, include:

In every moment, you are where you are supposed to be and there is an opportunity to serve, grow, and/or receive. The question is will you accept?

Every experience of life is a synchronistic-type encounter. There are no accidents or coincidences. Any form of assistance you offer is an act of healing for you, others, and the universe.

You will always receive help within an instance of sending forth a prayer. The question is, will you see it as such?

You must recognize that everything in your life is a part of answered prayer that has arisen from the depths of your soul.

Everything you do that is done consciously, is an act of power.

Affirmation:
I am quantum transformation expressing!

We Live in a Matrix of Downloadable Information

We live in a quantum field of resonant energy (the -Q- field) and inherent in that field are matrices (plural of matrix) of available and "downloadable" information – infinite potentials and possibilities – the evolutionary pulses that desire to create and evolve humankind and to give us a greater good. People like Jesus, Moses, Lao-Tze, Krishna, Buddha, and other great teachers were very connected to this evolutionary pulse and their lives revealed it. Each left a great legacy for the world, which came from information obtained from new matrices or grids of higher awareness.

A matrix is a collection of grids, such as the grids that identify where and how to move electricity from town to town; states have multiple matrix grids to carry electricity. A matrix of energetic information holds all types of different data or information – when the world was ready, several people got the idea for the radio – Marconi was just the first to take the "download" on the radio and turn it into a reality. The Wright brothers did it with the airplane, and so forth.

To be able to "download" information means that we, individually and/or collectively, have created a connection to an energetic impulse and how we work with the evolutionary pulse determines the value we receive from it. The matrix being shared with the world today contains fresh ideas on how to *BE* the ideals we espouse in the world; how to observe and *BE* present in everyday existence to the energies around us. This energy matrix supports a focus on the "now" moment, and is about clarity, focus, and being energetically pristine. Alignment with this energy calls us to *BE* and to engage with its presence, not next week when I know more, but NOW!

When we consciously engage with "now" energy, we have the capacity to witness what is energetically occurring and how we are showing up in the midst of what is occurring. We *BE* the witness to our behaviors and actions; we observe if we are acting out of a sense of anything less than Love (e.g., selfish, jealous...)

Quantum Workers in a Field of Infinite Potential

Understanding the implications of the -Q- field and its information has the potential for opening the way for a deeper comprehension of spiritual teachings. This enhanced understanding has the capacity to result in a continued evolution and enlightenment for individuals and society, alike.

Albert Einstein (among others) in his "Theory of Relativity" laid the groundwork for quantum revelation when he concluded that the entire universe is, at its most foundational and fundamental level, is composed of energy ($e=mc^2$). As energy, *Light,* is its highest form. Interestingly enough, in all major spiritual traditions there is a reference or teaching around Spirit/God/Essence as *Light*.

Hinduism refers to Lord/God, as warmth and *light*. The ancient Egyptian God Re, speaks of himself as the Lord of *Light*. In the *Torah,* there is a theme and thread that runs through it that refers to Spirit/God as Light. In Buddhism, *Light* envelopes the enlightened teacher. In the newly discovered *Nag Hammadi Library*, Gospel of Thomas, logion 50, Jesus refers to himself as, coming from the *Light* and being the image of that *Light*. The Sufi's proclaim, true knowledge comes from the *Light* and lastly, Christianity refers to the process of transfiguration as an act of being filled with *Light*.

From a psychological perspective, according to famous psychiatrist Carl Jung, enlightenment occurs when darkness (being unconscious or unskilled in our acts and behaviors) makes way for *Light* (recognizing and remembering through the revealing of our shadow aspects and being conscious of our acts and behaviors). It is *Light*, according to Jung, that is the energy that is released when our shadow aspects are freed up. Energy-Light-Spirit-Source, is it a coincidence the each of these words are interchangeable with the other and ultimately mean the same thing? Means the same thing, as in the mathematical equation: a=b, b=c, thus a=c. Does this interest you?

Jesus of Nazareth, among other spiritual teachers, was a creative partner with universal energies; he was a quantum-field worker. He understood the principles of quantum physics and used them for the good of humankind without ever having attended a class on quantum principles.

He performed his works utilizing the evolutionary pulse/ energy from the quantum field of consciousness. With it, he was able to shift the molecules in water and change them into wine. He called forth the spirit of Lazarus and raised him from the appearance of death. He spent six days on a mountain top in prayer, then returned illuminated by a light that emanated from within. He healed from a distance. He healed with a touch. He healed through the spoken word. He cast out negative energy. He left his physical body and then resurrected it and much more.

Jesus the Christ was a pioneer quantum physicist, a -Q- field worker without "specialized" training and/or, education; as was Moses, Isaiah, and other great spiritual teachers throughout the ages. What they did have, however, was a connection; a connection to a higher Source of information, knowledge, and awareness. For thousands of years spiritual teachers have worked earnestly to bring spiritual ideas into conscious awareness; however, much of the world was not ready for the information, many wanted a more scientific foundation. "Prove it and I will believe it – maybe." Now for those who need it scientifically, that proof is being given.

Our work as 21st century creative partners, working in this -Q- field of infinite potential, is to bring these evolutionary spiritual principles into conscious awareness and turn them into 'living' realities for everyday use; placing them into service for the greater good of the world.

How do we make these principles a living reality? It takes commitment to engage and work consciously with "truth" and with principle. It also takes a level of surrender and non-attachment to connect and work with the processes that have the capacity to shift our current realities and paradigms (sets of beliefs) and create quantum transformation in our lives.

The Impact of Conscious -Q- Creation (Quantum Physics, Choice and Intention)

"No matter how far down the wrong road
you have traveled, you can always turn back."
--Old Turkish Proverb

While research is revealing, that at the sub-atomic or quantum level, everything is interrelated and interconnected and that the fabric of reality is permeated with a substance that causes it to expand in response to a collection of thoughts, feelings, observations, etc. These research conclusions *support* the ancient and more recent spiritual teachings on the power of conscious choice and intention and their capacity to influence the conscious creation of results.

Spiritual teachings purport that intentions determine what is possible for our lives, because intentions are vehicles that help to transform universal energy into a "power" that infuses our thoughts and actions. However, the final result of the manifestation of our intention is intertwined with and influenced and determined by our beliefs and perceptions. To determine how our beliefs and perception influence the creation of our results, let us review again, their formation and function.

Beliefs are a collection of perceptions that have, in a sense, concretized. Perceptions are the filters through which we see reality and are created by the beliefs we hold. It is a circular type of existence; beliefs create the filters for perception and perceptions create the basis of beliefs. One influences and impacts the other and it just keeps going around until we make a conscious choice to change our beliefs.

If we make a conscious choice and create an intention around its outcome, we are initiating a process of conscious -Q- co-creation. However, many elements affect the final achievement of our results. The next two charts reveal how to work with and gain a sense of clarity around universal principles and the laws of manifestation and attraction in the conscious creation of results:

A "Mystery" Practice: The Art and Science of Intentional Creation

Consciously Creating Results
The Seven Levels of Intentional Creation

The Intentional Creation Process

*1. Idea:
>Light/Illumination
>Creation starts with an idea, through the involution of an energetic thought- idea an "internal light bulb" turns on in mind and we "see" something we have not "seen" before and we "call" it - idea!

>Explanation of Process
>Creation begins in the inner realms of being. Everything at the quantum level is interconnected through a web of string-like energy

that contains all knowledge and wisdom. We receive a "download" of energy that appears to us as a thought or a burst of light.

*2. Interpret:

Faith→Imagination

We take the "downloaded" idea and we interpret its value to us according to our current beliefs and perceptions. Imagination elicits attention and concentration as its partners and they support the creation of power-filled intentions when aligned with the feeling nature. We create images by means of words. Words express ideas- ideas create images and form a collective idea which forms our thought-habits that become the "power" of our mind.

Explanation of Process

Ideas travel this web of energy and come into our minds as thought-energy; this energy is moldable. At this point, the idea/ energy is completely neutral. Based upon our beliefs and perceptions we begin to assign interpretations to the idea/ thought-energy. It is through these interpretations that we begin to believe and put substance into our idea. Then our imagination, we will craft and mold new thoughts that will ultimately shape our experiences.

*3. Choice:

Understanding and Will

After we make our interpretation, seeing how the idea fits within our beliefs and perceptions; we start to give form in mind to our ideas, then we make a choice about what we will do with the information. e.g., we decide to use the idea and create an intention and/or an outcome for the idea, we choose to discard it or forget about it, or we choose to create Monkey Mind Chatter out of it – telling our selves how it will never work – because we are (I am) not worthy enough...

Explanation of Process

Our thoughts are energy and are the tools we create with and through. We live in an energetic -Q- universe and it is always ready to respond with a "YES" to the dominate thought-forms that we send forth. We create our dominate energetic thought-forms through our understanding and will, our perceptions and interpretations of our experiences. Through conscious choices, we continue to give shape to our thoughts.

*4. Intention:

Judgment and Discernment

Intention gives shapes to choices and the forms of imagination. We create intentions based on the choices we have and the discernment of the judgments we make. This gives power to our choices and further shape to the forms we are holding in mind – to that which we are giving our attention. Always intend that that which you are giving your concentrated attention to will manifest, NOW!

The Art of Attention and Intention:

It is time to enter into the Mysteries of the Mind and know that "I Am" is the Master of the Mind. The conscious mind must be tamed before you can get it to work properly. It loves to swing from subject to subject, when what is truly required is the power of attention.

Attention properly focused leads to power-filled intentions, for that to which the mind attends -carves the openings for dynamic interactions and intentions. The key is to attend to only one thing at a time – how do we do this when the world is so caught up in multi-tasking?

Actually, the mind cannot attend to more than one thing at a time. What appears as multi-tasking is the mind shifting rapidly from one neural pathway (thought or idea) to another. Purposeful, concentrated attention on an object or thought has the capacity to draw into the field of consciousness all the various ideas associated in memory and in the – Q- field of potential with the thought or object. Directed, concentrated attention carves or creates new channels for knowledge to flow through.

Attention increases the power of perception and brings into awareness the power of association, which is linked w/ memory recall. Attention and perception are "partners". The mind perceives not the senses, the mind perceives thru the senses and then registers what it sees. We receive thru our senses the impressions of the outside world, but the mind registers those perceptions as associated "feeling" memories.

When it appears that memory is failing, it is actually not the failing of memory but the slowing of the power of attention and association. Attention creates impressions and the stronger the impression received, the clearer the associative memory that supports the formation of recall and images (see Imagination). Do you see how circular this is?

Explanation of Process

As we create intentions for our choices remember – energy follows thought – and it is important to keep our intentions pure, to make judgments about why we are doing something.

What we send out as an intention for others will return to us in measure; thus, do not wish ill will for others. The highest intention intends that good and success come to all.

Affirmations help support our intentions, but negative thoughts that arise can negate our intentions, if we give them too much attention.

Be alert to the fact that, as humans, we have an addiction to being right. In order to be right, we tend to validate and justify our beliefs. We interpret through the filters of our beliefs (perceptions) and thus, create our experiences through those filters. When our beliefs/ perceptions get validated, we get to be "right".

Example: if we think someone does not like us we tend to hold back and be guarded when we are around them, perhaps we are even aloof and nasty. When they respond back to us in a manner that is unapproachable, unfriendly, detached, etc. we then can say – "See, I knew I was right, they don't like me." We created evidence to support our perception filters.

However, we do not see or are not honest about our initial behavior toward them; because we judged through our belief/perception that they didn't like us, we created an evidence and an opportunity to be right – to have our expectations met.

Simply stated, our thoughts and emotions shape our world and our arise from an invisible, quantum level.

As our thoughts and emotions arise, we assign meaning and value to them based upon an interpretation of them through our beliefs and perceptions. We then act upon – not the original thought but – our interpretation or perception of the thought we have "washed" through our belief-filters.

The universe then reflects back to us our "washed" thoughts; and we get to be "right" about that which we knew to be true in the first place. Do you get it?

The world, at times, is a mirror and spiritual feedback system that reflects our dominate thoughts, feelings, and intentions. We create our own issues and then get to live them, over and over, again – often thinking that someone else to blame.

Pain and suffering are a part of the soul's feedback mechanism; a way of letting us know that perhaps there is something *out of alignment*. Joy and peace are also a part of the soul's feedback; they let us know we are *in alignment* with our purpose and intention.

Are you ready for something new to happen in your life or some area of your life? Recreate new neural pathways. Change your thoughts and you will change your experiences!

*5. Feeling:

I Am

We imbue our intentions with positive feelings and thoughts. Feeling is a key to the process of creating. If we speak positive words and yet, feel uncertain and/or negative, about the outcome, the negative feeling will negate the positive thought.

The Infinite Mind holds all form ever though they are without form, we must give our thoughts form. Thru thinking we create, as we create images in our mind, we imbue our consciousness (perceptions, beliefs, etc.) into them.

Our images have only the power we imbue into them. Mind responds to vibrations of thought and thought is formed by our thinking and feeling natures. We have just begun to tap our inner resources and to discover our capacity to create.

The universe is ruled by Law, which is Principle in action. Law is the perfect pattern that IS in the Mind of Universal Being. An atom is a vortex of energy, of substance in motion, the *"coagulation of these vortices of force create matter according to the Law of Attraction which is incorporated... into the thought emanated."* Matter is a result of Mind and Energy in Action.

(ONE) Mind does however have different forms of manifestation, which are the Conscious and Sub-Conscious minds. Conscious mind is our way of contact with the physical world. In the subconscious mind lives instinctive mind, intellectual mind, and intuition mind with access to genius mind; 90% of all our mental operations are performed in the sub-conscious.

Our mind contains faculties which we have not yet unfolded but which are waiting for the human race to grow into. Jesus the Christ was a prototype and archetype for the expression of many of these yet un-awakened faculties and we are pioneers in their continuing evolution through the mind of humankind.

Imagine an iceberg, its tip is conscious mind and subconscious mind is large submerged base, and they both float in a sea of God Mind Substance.

Explanation of Process

Keep your thoughts and intentions connected to positive thoughts, faith, knowing that you have dominion and authority as creator. You can only feel less than, small or weak, when you are not connected to Source, your sense of wholeness, to your great I Am connection.

Continue to hold positive thoughts and feelings and the fabric of reality, the _Q_ field gets permeated with a substance that causes it to expand. It expands in response to not only observation, but also to our collective thoughts and feelings; which arise from our beliefs and perceptions. Do you see how this creative process is a circle that keeps turning back on itself?

NOTE:

On one hand our individual worlds are a reflection of our thoughts, by changing our beliefs, we change what we experience. We have the power to co-create, through our thoughts. We set intentions and create new experiences in accordance with our alignment with the laws and principles of attraction.

On the other hand, life is impersonal. Things happen to us that we have no control over and that are not necessarily our fault or responsibility (e.g., drunk drivers).

Life doesn't always show up in the way we expect it to, yet, we are still in control to choose what we create. What we have the power to create, though, is our *response* to what is happening. How we respond has a direct correlation to how connected we are to Source Energy.

What happens in the world is not as important as *how we respond to* what is happening. Our responses work as an attractor, as a magnet to bring back to us that which we have put out as a thought and intention through our responses to situations. Most everything we do in life has a decision, a choice-moment, attached to it. We have the power to decide and choose how we will express (respond) to our thoughts and experiences through our choices – will I, in this moment, choose to respond from love or fear? We make the decision as to how we will respond to what we see – not someone else. We are not victims of life. We are purpose-oriented, _Q_ accountable, choice-makers, this is who we have come here to BE. Life is impersonal – things happen – get over them – don't make them your god!

*6. Release:

Rest in Realization

When we are in alignment with the –Q– field, we can easily release the specifics of our intention-knowing, trusting, and surrendering -all the while being patient, grateful, and yet non-attached to the outcome.

Why do metaphysicians always stress that we should be willing to release. As was stated, imagine an iceberg, its tip is conscious mind and subconscious mind is large submerged base, and they both float in a sea of God Mind Substance.

Together they create form and manifest in the visible world. Yet one day everything they created will slide back into the One Great Sea of Mind Substance from which they originally sprang forth. Release and Let Go, it is all temporary, anyway!

Explanation of Process
Give the thought-intention time to imprint upon the energetic fabric of the universe and to mature. Hold it in prayer, affirm it, have faith in it, work with it, and give it space to ripen. Be alert to staying positive and true to the intended outcome – do not go off on negative tangents.

Go into the silence, or sit in quiet contemplation until you feel a "quickening" or a feeling of oneness with the unified field. At this point, when there is a sense of energetic connection, speak your affirmation into the unified resonant field of energy that surrounds you and from which your ideas take form.

This is different from just verbalizing an affirmation for whatever it is you want. This is consciously connecting with the energy of the resonant unified field that we live and move in. When we do this, we are allowing the energetic field to use us. We are not using the field and this is important for the highest manifestation of good for all. Then release the outcome, as in non-attachment to outcome, knowing that it may not unfold as expected; but it will be right and perfect for all involved. Gratitude is a balm to the soul and opens the way for the highest good of all involved to be revealed and realized.

*7. Action:
Imagine you can do it, begin to act it out in your life –even if you can't see it happening yet- this creates a Habit of BE-ing. We put feelings into our intention, then we take authentic action/s as guided, knowing that conscious choices aligned with intentions and imbued with positive feelings get imprinted upon the universal substance and manifest accordingly! Think and Act in harmony!

Explanation of Process
Listen, listen, listen, and listen some more. Continue to return and connect with the energy of the unified field. All has be given, it needs time to manifest or be demonstrated. Move as guided, nudged, or directed by universal energy (God, Spirit, Higher Power...) as heard through the act of listening.

A living reality will manifest, your intention will bear fruit in accordance with the primary or dominate thoughts held in your mind and heart.

A "Mystery" Practice:
Intentional Creation Results in Alignment with the Evolutionary Pulse

The following is a chart that supports our efforts in conscious intentional – Q- creation. On the right side of the chart are tools that sustain us in the unfolding of the creative process – the evolutionary pulse; on the left side of the chart are ways that we often tend to sabotage our efforts.

Read the ideas on the left and ask yourself if these are thoughts that tend to arise when you start to create a goal, or desire a specific outcome for your life. If you feel a twinge or "knowing" that this behavior, belief, or action is one that you to engage in, then move to the column on the right and read the supporting affirmation.

Start to plant the affirmation as a seed by reading it 3 times a day for 21 days. This action will begin to grow the seed affirmation and help to support you in consciously replacing and overcoming the "old" behavior, action, or belief.

Commitment to participation in the acts of self-observation and self-honesty are pre-requisites to effectively working with the creative process.

Conscious Intentional -Q- Creation:
Intentional Creation Results in Alignment with the Evolutionary Pulse

Thoughts, Beliefs, Behaviors, and Attitudes That Slow the Flow of Creative Energy and Sabotage Our Efforts	Thoughts, Beliefs, Behaviors, and Attitudes That Increase the Flow of Creative Energy and Enhance Our Efforts
I think I want this, but, what if...	I am in alignment when I am clear that:
I think, maybe, I might want that, perhaps I do! I am wishy-washy, unclear on what I want.	I am a creator with universal energy; this energy is moldable and responds to my thoughts.
I believe that in order to get what I want I must help things along by controlling and manipulating my environment and/or people.	I know universal energy supports the highest and best outcome for all involved and I let go!
I am clear and I am still afraid I may not get what I want. I need this...	I know that energy follows thoughts. I am focused and have clarity regarding the outcome of my intentions.

I dwell on: What if I don't get this ... I am not smart enough...I don't have enough to...I don't know enough people to...

I think, maybe, that someone else deserves this more than me, after all, I haven't ...I don't...Why would I...

I insist on holding on, trying to force my outcome on ... I demand you see it my way!

I am afraid! If (insert) doesn't happen I won't get ...

I need this don't you understand. If I don't get this...

I said my affirmations and I know I should be positive but, you don't understand what this means to me, what if...?

Heck with him/her, so what if they lose a little bit or don't get promoted, I got mine!

Perhaps if I... Go to the boss and tell him/her... Put a little pressure on them, it will happen...

I am an emotional basket case, if I don't get what I want I will...

I am afraid... I felt the nudge, but couldn't follow through...

Heck with them, I deserve this...

I know that my thoughts and intentions are in alignment with my soul's purpose – which is to grow in conscious awareness.

I know that I am worthy to receive.

I release any pre-conditioned ideas as to the outcome of my intentions.

I trust the process and have faith in the perfect outcome for all involved.
I am grateful for the perfect outcome and can release how it must manifest.
I consciously imbue my intention/s with positive thoughts. I am aware of thoughts that arise that are not of the same vibration!

I affirm the greater good of all involved.

I surrender the process and outcome and allow divine timing to unfold the greater good for all involved.

I am aligned with positive feelings and thoughts, now!

I take authentic actions as guided.

I am grateful.

| Uhh? What? I do that most of the time…why should I change, let them change. | I know that my thoughts are things and shape the circumstances of my life. My experiences act as a spiritual feedback system and I am alert to what they revealing back to me. |

A "Mystery" Practice: The Keys to Intentional Creation

For this practice, we are going to have one (1) minute to respond to each segment. Why do we have only one minute for each segment? When we take too much time to think about a question and then, it's right answer, our mind starts engaging in monkey-mind chatter and often takes us off course. One minute to respond, keeps us focused and on purpose. In addition, with a short response time, we tend to by-pass the frivolous and move into the 'juice' of what really wants to be exposed.

<u>Question:</u>   What experiences have repeatedly shown up in your life; focus in the areas of relationship issues, financial struggles, health problems, family situations, prosperity, and/or education?
Take only one (1) minute to respond. If this is a group setting share your one minute response with a partner. If you are alone, begin to talk, perhaps into a mirror – but time yourself – and when you have completed the one minute, stop and write what you remember of your responses in a journal. Remember; take only one (1) minute. What do you notice?

<u>Question:</u>   Are you ready to create a more conscious life?
Answer either: "Yes" or "No."
If yes, take one (1) minute, to list what would be included in your life if it was intentional and on purpose? List not only what would be in your life; but also, who you would be as you lived it, and what would have to change or transform within you for this to happen.
Take only one (1) minute to respond. If this is a group-setting share your one minute response with a partner. If you are alone, begin to talk, perhaps into a mirror – but time your self – and when you have completed the one minute, stop and write what you remember of your responses in a journal.
Take only one (1) minute.   What do you notice?
To live an intentional life we consciously choose to focus on the <u>S</u>ource of who we are, our magnificence, not our perceived "short-comings". We remember that any expression that is revealing its self through us – as work, desire for success, motherhood, writer, etc. – is only a transitory expression.

<u>Creating Conscious Intentions</u>   Using the previous exercises as a foundation, now create a conscious intention that reflects the intent of what you want to say, "YES" to in your life – what you really want to experience.
Take only one (1) minute to create this intention. Start your statement with, "As a conscious co-creator of my life I choose to …" If this is a group-setting share your statement with a partner. If you are alone, begin to talk, perhaps into a mirror – but time your self – and when you have completed the one minute, stop and write what you remember of your responses in a journal. Remember; take only (1) minute. What do you notice?

Chapter 5
BE! at Work in Our Professional Life

> *"The cultures of corporations, government institutions,*
> *and non-governmental agencies are a direct reflection*
> *of the consciousness of the current leaders*
> *and the legacy of past leaders...*
> *Cultural transformation begins with the*
> *personal transformation of the leaders and*
> *building group cohesion in the leadership team."* [46]
> --Richard Barrett

> *"Today's business and world leaders are faced with unprecedented*
> *complexities and rates of change in markets and social conditions.*
> *This places extreme pressure on leaders to develop all aspects of*
> *themselves to the highest degree possible.*
> *Development of their cognitive, emotional, interpersonal, and ethical*
> *capacities, as well as their fundamental sense of self, and more,*
> *are all required. In my opinion, only those who*
> *develop to this level, who integrate fully to this level,*
> *will be successfully equipped to manage a profitable,*
> *sustainable growth business or effective organization."* [47]
> *– Ken Wilber*

-Q- Oriented Organizations: A Myth or Possible Reality?

In this chapter, through the introduction of developmental theories (leadership, whole-person, and more) and best standards of organizational practices, we continue our journey of "conscious living" with a focus on how to BE! in the work environment.

As we make our passage through the information presented in this chapter, please note that the models, concepts, and theories discussed are initiatory introductions to specific bodies of knowledge. The presentations of the various models, etc. are designed to spark interest and awareness in the subject matter and are not to be considered as in-depth teachings.

Each model presented has an underpinning body of knowledge and a pioneering developer, master teacher, and/or certified teachers that present the depth and breadth of the models design.

Thus, the information provided in this chapter (and in this book) is intended to sprinkle seeds of excitement within the reader, in the hopes that the seeds will grow into a desire to:

---

[46] Barrett, Richard. *Liberating the Corporate Soul.* Butterworth-Heinemann. San Francisco, CA. 1998
[47] Wilber, Ken. *A Theory of Everything.* Shambala Press. Boston, MA.

- Delve further into research of the subject matter presented.
- Entice the reader to explore stage specific coaching and goal creation.
- Explore a more in-depth review of state and stage transition challenges.
- Create new strategies and structures for personal and professional developmental growth and awareness (leadership, whole-person, etc.).
- Discover tools to aid in the transition to the next state, stage, and/or level of awareness.

To This Point We Have Pondered:

Up to this point in the book we have immersed ourselves in the inquiry of:

- What does it mean to dance at the edge of mystery?
- What is the –Q- field and integral concept?.
- What does it mean to create intentional conscious choices?
- What does it mean to notice, and be interested in what is energetically arising in the moment?
- What is the gift we receive from being willing to sit in the question vs. always needing answers?
- What is shadow-stuff? What does it mean and how do we participate in conscious clean up in consciousness (shadow-dancing)?
- What is the creative power of "YES?"
- What does it mean to participate in conscious living?
- What is the state of *BE?*
- What is the relationship between quantum concepts and spiritual principles, and their correlation with conscious -Q- creation?.
- How do the ideas, theories, models, views, beliefs, and concepts presented relate to, impact, and influence the unfolding of our human potential?

How Do We Consciously Develop Human Potential?

Continuing in this vain of uncovering, discovering, and unfolding human potential let us turn to sociological and developmental researchers for information that can support us in our journey of consciously bringing transformation and "spiritual" growth into the work environment.

Researchers and teachers such as, Susan Cook-Greuter, William Tolbert, Ken Wilber, Clare Graves, David Cooperrider, Don Beck, Cindy Wigglesworth, Abraham Maslow, and many, many others have created development theory models that describe in some manner or fashion the process of the unfolding of human potential.

Their findings and writings reveal that with each state and stage of unfoldment of human potential (states are temporary, while stages of consciousness are permanent and represent the actual milestones of growth and development), a person moves towards a deeper understanding, wisdom and effectiveness in the world arena.

Development theories provide a way of understanding how people tend to interpret events, and how they are likely to act in many common and uncommon situations. Susan Cook-Greuter, leadership and whole-person development expert, purports (her original thoughts have been adapted here by William R. Torbert, *Action Inquiry* and creator of Torbert's Action Logic);

"Development occurs through the interplay between person and environment, not just by one or the other. It is a potential that can be encouraged and facilitated by appropriate support and challenge... Growth occurs in a logical sequence of stages or expanding world-views from birth to adulthood. The journey is often likened to an ever-widening spiral.

Development in its deepest meaning refers to transformations of consciousness – in perspectives, paradigms, worldviews, and mental models. A person's worldview/ frame/ stage of development influences what they notice or can become aware of - and therefore what they can describe, articulate, influence, and change.

Although a person may use several perspectives in a day, we tend to prefer to respond spontaneously with the most complex meaning-making system, perspective, or mental model we have mastered. This preferred perspective is called a person's "center of gravity" or their "central meaning-making tendency."

It's important to distinguish between lateral and vertical development. Both are important, but they occur at different rates. Lateral growth and expansion (within a stage) happens through many channels, such as schooling, training, self-directed and life-long learning as well as simply through exposure to life.

Vertical development (from stage to stage) in adults is rarer. It refers to how we learn to see the world through new eyes, how we change our interpretations of experience, and how we transform our views of reality. It describes shifts in what we are aware of, and what we can pay attention to - and therefore how we can lead and what we can manage, as well as what we can influence and integrate."

Organizations consist of individuals and each individual adds to the collective mind-set or consciousness of the organization. Leaders set the tone of the organization and that tone is directly related to their state and stage of development on the ever-evolving spiral of human values and conditions. This chapter (and book) is dedicated, albeit very simplistically, to sharing new thoughts, ideas, and information on how an individual can create transformations and shifts within themselves; it is not necessarily easy work, but it can be done! All paradigm shifts, started with one person, somewhere, believing in some idea or ideal.

In 1982 Ken Keyes, wrote a book about paradigm shifts, using a concept he entitled, the 100th monkey syndrome. Keyes purported that when a new idea surfaces and people start to utilize and/or believe in the idea and then put the idea into practice; a shift in consciousness will occur. The new idea has a created a paradigm shift, a major shift in the awareness of society. The shift has moved a previously unknown concept or idea into the mainstream of society; this is what happened with the use of computers. Think about the telephone, one hundred years ago they were non-existent, yet, could we live without them now?

The paradigm shift occurs as a result of a critical mass of people believing in and engaging in working with a new concept, idea, or ways of being and doing. Critical mass means that a sufficient number of people (no one really knows what that number is) have taken the concept, idea, etc. and put it to use. The concept, etc. now becomes a new paradigm or belief set.

The impact that these concepts of critical mass and paradigm shift have for the work environment is that when enough people get behind an idea or change their mind about an idea, person, or project happening within the system, they have the capacity to shift, change or transform the system in accordance with their new belief set. However, it works both ways; the shift can work to create positive energy or negative. What we would like to have happen in our organizations is for these conversations that lead to shifts in awareness, to be forward moving and positive in nature.

A foundational underpinning that exists in both quantum physics and spiritual teachings is that the universe is an interactive system in which changes in one part influence the other parts, even across great distances. Our work is to learn how to put this principle into use for the greater good of all within life and business. This chapter is dedicated to doing just that!

A Changing Epistemology

> *"A human being is a part of a whole, called by us universe...*
> *He experiences himself, his thoughts and feelings*
> *as something separated from the rest ...*
> *a kind of optical delusion of his consciousness.*
> *The delusion is a ... prison for us,*
> *restricting us to our personal desires*
> *and to affection for a few persons nearest to us.*
> *Our task must be to free ourselves from this prison*
> *by widening our circle of compassion*
> *to embrace all living creatures*
> *and the whole of nature and its beauty."*
> --Albert Einstein

What constitutes a -Q- organization and defines -Q- leadership"? To have quantum organizations requires that key leaders be committed to living transformational practices, personally and professionally. The thing about principle is that principles (spiritual or otherwise) are of no practical value, unless there is integration of the principles into consciousness and everyday awareness. Without conscious integration, principles are just intellectual concepts that we have accumulated within the confines of our mind space. As Gandhi shared, "We must *BE* the change we want to see".

Epistemology is the branch of philosophy that investigates the nature, limits, criteria, and validity of human knowledge. For over 200 years there has been a prevailing epistemology based upon a theory set forth by Sir Isaac Newton. This knowledge, known as, Newtonian Law or Newtonian Perspectives has worked effectively; in fact, its principles took us to the moon.

The current discovery that has the greatest potential for an epistemological influence is that of quantum physics. Quantum physics is the study of how the universe operates at the quantum or sub nuclear level; a realm invisible to the naked eye. However, it is as real as that which we see daily with our eyes and perceive through our minds, and perhaps more so. Quantum physics is adding another dimension to Newton's findings, for it is an emerging epistemology that has the potential to be transformative to the conduct of life and all it entails, including the transaction of business.

Newton discovered the law of gravity, as he sat under an apple tree. (We have to ask, was this event an accident or synchronicity?) Newton's discovery confirmed that the universe does indeed operate through immutable, undeniable, and irrefutable universal laws and principles. These laws allow for the development of verifiable theories. Mathematics is one of these immutable laws, two plus two will always equal four (2+2=4); no matter how much we might want it to equal seven (7).

Newtonian verifiable theories, however, lead to ideas and ideals grounded in an intellectual knowledge that has become, perceived by some as, concrete and immovable. Quantum theories, are thought to be grounded in interconnection, change, chaos as part of shift, self-organizing patterns, and much more. As quantum principles become part of the everyday culture and consciousness, they too will create paradigm shifts in ways of leadership, just as Newtonian theories did. These shifts will affect our ways of being; and these ways of being will create changes in our personal and professional lives. The following are examples!

Whole- Brained -Q- Organizations

"...Organizational change happens one person at a time.
Our workplace simply mirrors our individual and collective beliefs.
Therefore, we change, ourselves, our workplaces,
and the world by changing our minds.
As our beliefs change, we not only see the world differently,
we begin to be in the world in a different way,
thus creating a new reality."[48]
--Charlotte Shelton

It is said that -Q- organizations are whole-brained[49] organizations; meaning that both the right and left hemispheres of the brain of the organization (for an organization is a 'living' entity) are in balance in the process of modeling and managing.

In such an organization, the qualities and attributes of both right-brain and left-brain focus are honored and respected. Qualities of left-brain focus include understanding the rules of commerce and business; having defined vision, mission, and core values; working from a plan of strategic intentions; policies and procedures are in place; etc.

The qualities and attributes of a right-brain focus are; empathy, caring, compassion, flexibility, creativity and creative expression, diversity of people and perspectives, and an appreciation of the potential that chaos can bring forth when dialogue is permitted in the midst of chaos.

The -Q- organization is one that works in tandem with the two hemispheres allowing each to lead when needed or necessary. It is open to change and shift and permitting that change to happen quickly and nearly effortlessly. It is a company where all persons have an emotional stake in the company; not just shareholders or executive boards. All come together to share ideas and ideals.

Author and corporate values guru, Richard Barrett[50] espouses this type of creative effort when he invites the whole of a corporation to come together and help define its core values. To have such -Q- organizations requires leaders who are committed to personal transformation, not only for themselves but for all who work within their environment.

---

[48] Shelton, Charlotte. *Quantum Leaps: 7 Skills for Workplace ReCreation*. Butterworth-Heinemann. Boston, MA.
[49] Shelton, Charlotte. *Quantum Leaps: 7 Skills for Workplace ReCreation*. Butterworth-Heinemann. Boston, MA. pg.9
[50] Barrett, Richard. *Building a Values-Driven Organization*. Elsevier. San Francisco. 2006

A "Mystery" Practice: Comparing Newtonian Mechanistic With Quantum(-Q-) Living Systems

We have discussed in general, the conceptual differences in Newtonian vs. Quantum "Living" systems, now let us review the specific differences. The following is a chart that compares the Newtonian/Mechanistic/Left-Brain Oriented system of thinking, with its counterpart -Q-/'Living' System/Right-Brain Oriented system of thinking.

Organizational consultant, Susan Burnett-Hampson, created the chart from a synthesis of ideas collected from various authors on the subject, along with her own input. It is interesting to see the views side by side and then compare them, not as in judgment, but in how each one adds to the creation of the collective health and consciousness of both individuals and organizations.

"Comparison" Practice Directions:

On the chart below, peruse the attributes contained within each directory. Be cognizant of what you notice around each pair of words and what the words create as a "stir" or feeling, if any. Sit with the both component pieces and consider how each one has the potential to impact your life and/or an organization. As you ponder the consequences of each, consider how the use of them (or not) is currently affecting you personally and professionally and especially as to how you live and/or do business from that particular mind set, behavior, or attitude, or not. Look for and be open to new possibilities and new perspectives on being, modeling, and leading.

After you have completed reviewing the chart, select three sets of attributes that have "stirred" something within you. List the three and then record what it is that they have elicited as an awareness or insight as to how you use them now or how you can create a behavioral or attitudinal shift – either in everyday life or in your work environment.

After completing this, select the one that you feel is most important to you and if you are alone, delve deeper into its insight and meaning through journaling – continually asking yourself what you are noticing about the word and/or insight. If you are in a group setting, share your insights with a partner.

Chart: A Comparison of Newtonian and $-Q-$ Living Systems

CHART BY SUSAN BURNETT-HAMPSON

Newtonian/Mechanistic Left-Brain Oriented Thinking	Quantum/Living Systems Right-Brain Oriented Thinking
*SEPARATE COMPARTMENTS	*HOLOGRAPHIC; ALL PARTS INTERRELATED
*CAUSE AND EFFECT AS FUNDAMENTAL	*BOTH CHAOTIC AND SELF-ORGANIZING
*OBJECTIVE OBSERVERS	*VIEWERS AS PARTICIPANTS
*ANALYTICAL	*SYNTHESIS
*REDUCTIONIST	*MYSTERY
*STATIC	*CONSTANT FLUX
*EITHER/OR	*BOTH/AND
*POLARITIES	*PARADOX/ NO RIGHT OR WRONG
*EARTH/COSMOS AS OBJECT	*EARTH/COSMOS AS ORGANISM
*EQUILIBRIUM PREFERRED STATE	*EQUILIBRIUM = DEATH
*STANDARDIZED STRUCTURE: APPLIED TO ALL SITUATIONS	*SYSTEMS INDIVIDUALIZED; FIT NEED OF MOMENT
*INTELLIGENT STRATEGIES	*NOVEL PATTERNS W/INFINITE VARIETY
*INTELLIGENT STRATEGIES MUST BE "FIGURED OUT" WITH OUR MINDS	*INTUITION AND DISCERNMENT + MIND
*"AFFLUENZA"	*"LESS IS MORE"
*"HUMAN-CENTRIC"	*CREATION-CENTRIC
*DOING-CENTERED; TASK ORIENTED	*BEING CENTERED; CONVERSATIONS ARE THE TOOL OF CREATIVITY
*CONTROL	*TRUST
*1 + 1 = 2 (PERIOD)	*1 + 1 = 2 AND WHO KNOWS WHAT ELSE?
*MISTAKES = FAILURE; TO BE AVOIDED	*MISTAKES = SUCCESS; CREATE SAFE SPACE TO MAKE THEM
*CHAOS = DESTRUCTION	*CHAOS = CREATIVITY
*LARGE OUTER INTERVENTIONS VEHICLES FOR MAJOR CHANGE	*SMALL, ISOLATED VARIATIONS CAN PRODUCE HUGE EFFECTS
*CONTROL; HIERARCHY AS ONLY OPERATING SYSTEM	*SELF-ORGANIZING INTELLIGENCE
*SOME PARTS/JOBS MORE IMPORTANT THAN OTHERS AND HOLD MORE WEIGHT	*EVERY VOICE MATTERS; NOT ONLY ARE ALL PARTS IMPORTANT, THEY ARE NECESSARY FOR THE WHOLE

Two World Views

After reviewing the different aspects of the Newtonian and –Q-perspectives, it is becoming evident that we (humankind) are preparing for and/or are in the midst of a paradigm shift in consciousness. This evolution has shifted and will continue to shift what constitutes acceptable behaviors in the world and in standard business practices.

New models of personal-professional interaction provide innovative skill-sets that present new possibilities for ways of being in the work environment. Leaders can no longer assume that because they said so, people will follow what they say. Human Resource departments assure that employees receive respect and dignity and that grievances have a channel for honest expression. People are changing; they no longer want to be seen as predictable; as once in a job always in the same job until they retire; as machines to be worked until they break, then discarded, like an old shoe. As the world evolves so does the perspective of businesses need to evolve in alignment with it.

Author, Charlotte Shelton[51] asserts that quantum physics is a better metaphor for human behavior than that of the classic, Newtonian physics; due to the narrow, mechanistic approach of the Newtonian view, which creates limited potential within both life and the work environment.

Quantum principles, aligned with spiritual principles (e.g., each person has an inherent spark of divinity within them and thus are by nature, good) is one of the proto-types for the emergence of new business values. Quantum transformational processes are a resource that are just beginning to be tapped in regards to the depth of what they hold as potential and possibility for change within our systems and organizations.

This information being provided is not meant to be an either/or; meaning that we are advocating the throwing out of all Newtonian perspectives and replacing them with quantum theories and ideas. Newtonian perspectives have a place in business, they are useful in problem solving and error detecting, which, ultimately helps to increase standards and standards of practice.

A "Mystery" Practice: Two World Views

The Two World Views[52] chart, referenced below, was developed by Shelton and gives another simple and clear-cut analysis of the differences between the Newtonian and Quantum views of the world. As you review the chart, be interested and notice what differences you see in the potential for

51 Shelton, Charlotte. *Quantum Leaps*. Butterworth-Heinemann. Boston, MA. pg. 4
52 Shelton, Charlotte. *Quantum Leaps*. Butterworth-Heinemann. Boston, MA. pg. 4

valuing people inherent in each of the two views. Journal your thoughts regarding the differences; then think about which perspective works in what types of situations and under what types of conditions in the work environment. e.g., in the military, leaders directives are to be respected and heeded, or great chaos might ensue.

Two World Views Chart

FROM A NEWTONIAN PERSPECTIVE THE WORLD IS:	FROM A QUANTUM PERSPECTIVE THE WORLD IS:
MATERIAL, VISIBLE, CONCRETE STATIC, STABLE,	INTANGIBLE, INVISIBLE, ABSTRACT DYNAMIC, VIBRATING, IN CONTINUOUS CHANGE
PASSIVE, INERT	A SELF-ORGANIZING SYSTEM, CHAORDIC
PREDICTABLE, CONTROLLABLE UNAFFECTED BY OBSERVATION; REALITY IS OBJECTIVE	UNPREDICTABLE, INDETERMINATE AFFECTED BY THE CONSCIOUSNESS OF THE OBSERVER; REALITY IS SUBJECTIVE
A MACHINE; THINGS ARE BEST UNDERSTOOD BY REDUCING THEM TO THEIR SIMPLEST PARTS;	A SYSTEM; EVERYTHING IS PART OF AN INTER- RELATED WHOLE;
THE PARTS DETERMINE THE WHOLE	THE WHOLE DETERMINES THE PARTS
CONTROLLED LOCALLY; CAUSE AND EFFECT CLEARLY DISCERNED	AFFECTED BY MUCH MORE THAN MEETS THE EYE; THINGS HAPPEN 'FROM A DISTANCE
DEPENDENT UPON EXTRINSIC ENERGY SOURCES; WITHOUT EXTERNAL FORCE THINGS FALL APART	FILLED WITH ENERGY; ENERGY IS INTRINSIC TO LIFE AND ITS SYSTEMS

CHART BY CHARLOTTE SHELTON, PH.D.

Shelton then takes the foundational ideals and ideas of a two-world view and applies them, in the following chart, to reveal how each view or perspective is utilized within the organization setting.

Please note: all charts used in this book, not created by the author, are used with written permission of the original author/s.

Two Organizational Views Chart[53]

Newtonian/Mechanistic View *Organizations are:*	*Quantum/"Living" Systems View* *Organizations are:*
1. Much like a machine; machines are constructed of precise, standardized parts; they are therefore, structure-oriented.	1. Living organisms with no two identical parts, they are, therefore, process-oriented.
2. Static, stable, passive, inert.	2. Dynamic, continuously changing.
3. Predictable; they function according to a linear chain of cause-and-effect; breakdowns are readily identifiable.	3. Unpredictable; they function according to cyclical patterns of information (feedback loops); breakdowns caused by interaction of multiple factors.
4. Externally controlled; close observation is required.	4. Self-organizing; order is created internally, autonomy is required.
5. Best understood by reducing them to their simplest parts; the parts determine the whole.	5. Best understood by observing the whole; the whole determines the parts.
6. Closed systems; proceed toward entropy.	6. Open systems; continuously interact with the environment; evolve to ever higher levels of order and complexity; they self-renew and self-transcend.

Chart by Charlotte Shelton, Ph.D.

Shelton purports that in self-organizing, open systems, change emerges and is welcomed. Change is perceived as possibility, the gift that evolves out of creative and innovative act of participants sitting in the mystery and calling forth the next questions and the next step/s. In open systems, ideas bubble up, rather than being thrust down through the ranks, from the top. Additionally, empowerment of the whole system emerges from a sense of trust and openness and these ideals can only evolve out of organizations that are coherent systems. A little further, on in this chapter, we will look at what it means to be a coherent organization.

---

[53] Shelton, Charlotte. *Quantum Leaps.* Butterworth-Heinemann. Boston, MA. pg. 130.

Problem Solving vs. Positive Solution Model

Working to create practical and innovate solutions, we now move to how our two-views (Newtonian and -Q-) can be placed in a framework regarding how each serves in the problem-solving arena of the work environment. Problems, issues, challenges, etc., are inherent in the activity of daily living in a work environment, so the question is not – do problems exist within an organization? But, how can we respond to these problems and do it in a way that is mature and evolved?

In reviewing potential answers to this "problem/issues" aspect of business, which by the way, every company faces, a model that supports our two-view theory is by psychologist, Steve Lankton. His model is entitled: *Historical-Psychological Problem Solving Model vs. the Quantum-'Living' Systems, Positive-Solution Oriented Model.* The model is self-explanatory and is in alignment with the other models we have reviewed. As we review the model, remember, "What do you notice about yourself in each of these models and what about that do you find interesting about what you are noticing?"

Problem-Solving Model vs. Positive-Solution Model Chart

The Historical–Psychological Problem-Solving Oriented Model	The Quantum "Living" Systems Positive-Solution Oriented Model
Basic Assumption:	**Basic Assumption:**
I see there is a problem that needs to be resolved or a person that is an issue.	The situation or person is a mystery, let us embrace it and discover what desires to be birthed.
I ask about and look for all the problems and issues.	I ask what is working and has worked in the past?
I begin to label the problems.	I look for resolutions and answers that already exist.
I unconsciously focus on limitation and lack, when I label.	I focus on the positive and that which will create energy.
I work to fix what is out of order or in disarray.	I increase and strengthen what is already working and positive.
I find out who is to blame. I learn from errors, fault- finding, and inadequacies.	I see whom I can affirm. I learn from what works.

Adapted by Steve Lankton, Ph.D.

This chart is a tool that can be utilized both on an individual and collective basis. It can be used to assess not only the types of skills we use as a leaders, managers, and employees but also, whether the skills we use evolve from a problem-solver view or a positive-solution creator view. Remember, neither model is meant to be seen as right nor wrong, they can each be utilized, depending upon the situation or condition.

A "Mystery" Practice: Creative Solutions

Problem-solving is important to the day-to-day operations of any organization. This exercise is about learning how to shift our orientation so that when we problem-solve, no one "has to get" blamed or shamed when something does not work out perfectly or according to plan. There are alternative, creative solutions for problem solving that can create win/win/win situations for all involved – even if the goal was not achieved or attained.

This practice can be adapted for an individual or a group work.

Think of a situation in which you were involved, where you used the factors found in the problem-solving approach and the focus ended up being that someone was made wrong or someone got blamed for the situation or condition.

Make a note of the general particulars of the situation. If in a group, share the situation with a partner; if you are alone write about the details in your journal.

Now, review the positive-oriented solutions, consider how you might have shifted the focus in your specific situation, and created a more positive-solution orientation to the incidence for the person or people involved?

What would had to shift within you or your management team in order to create a more positive-oriented solution or, an interaction that felt more like a win/win/win for all involved?

If in a group, pair up and discuss your newfound possibilities, one person at a time; if you are alone journal your responses.

After you have completed sharing or writing, what do notice? Do you notice any shifts in your awareness and/or new possibilities for approaching situations that you might use at another time?

Positive-oriented solutions arise out of the art of asking "right" questions; let us now turn to a model that teaches us what "right" questions are and how we can create right and positive-oriented questions.

Appreciative Inquiry and the Art of Asking "Right" Questions

21st century leadership guru and organizational consultant, David Cooperrider, Ph.D., has created a model known as "Appreciative Inquiry" (a.k.a., AI).

AI *"...is an organizational development process or philosophy that engages individuals with an organizational system in its renewal, change, and focused performance."* [54]

Cooperrider, a professor at Case Western Reserve University in Ohio, created his work from concepts held by earlier theorists on similar subjects. AI is accepted as a best practice in the evaluation of organizational developmental and effectiveness strategies.

What is special about AI is the way it has of creating positive relationships as part of its organizational curriculum. AI's strength is that it envisions the future through calling upon positive events of the past, and thus builds a rapport for the future through a positive approach to change. By calling upon positive past events and then using them to create a "now", awareness the organization builds upon its strengths in order to co-create a future. According to Cooperrider AI is a:

"... systematic discovery of what gives a system 'life' when it is most effective and capable in economic, ecological, and human terms... involves the art and practice of asking questions that strengthen a system's capacity to heighten positive potential.

It mobilizes inquiry through crafting an 'unconditional positive question'... the arduous task of intervention gives way to the speed of imagination and innovation; instead of negation, criticism, and spiraling diagnosis, there is discovery, dream, and design... [in each person there is a] "positive change core"— and it assumes that every living system has many untapped and rich and inspiring accounts of the positive.

Link the energy of this core directly to any change agenda and changes never thought possible are suddenly and democratically mobilized." [55]

One aspect of AI is that it teaches how to formulate and ask "right" questions. Through "right" questioning, it is purported that awareness shifts through the act of a more positive type of inquiry and that results in a potential for a more positive state of change or shift in a person or situation. "Right questions" are positive results-oriented questions and include, but are not limited to those such as the following:

---

[54] Cooperrider, David. *Appreciative Inquiry*. Wikipedia. www.wikepedia.com

[55] Cooperrider, D.L. and Whitney, D., *"Appreciative Inquiry: A positive revolution in change."* In P. Holman and T. Devane (eds.), The hange Handbook, Berrett-Koehler Publishers, Inc., pages 245-263.

The Art of Asking Positive-Solution Oriented Questions

- "What possibilities exist that I have not thought about yet?"

- "What is the smallest change that I could make that would have the biggest impact on my life?"

- "What solutions could I/we make that would be a win/win/win for everyone involved?" (This means: I win and you win and out of both of us winning, a third ""synergistic-type win" evolves that is bigger than what was dreamed of originally.)

- "Are my questions inspiring, energizing, and mobilizing?"

- "What have I done right in my life?"

- "How can I continue to build upon my "right" experiences?"
- "Am I ready to learn the lesson that life and its experiences are trying to reveal to me?"

- "Am I willing and ready to shift, change, and grow?"

- "Am I ready to make a conscious choice?"

- "Am I engaging consciously in this situation and in the experiences of my life?"

- "What did I/we learn from the situation?"

- "What did I contribute to the situation, condition, or person?"

- "How can I best respond in the future, if this situation arises
- again?"

- "Who am I?" "What do I believe?" and "How am I living those beliefs, or not?"

Questions to Reflect Upon:
*What do you notice about having asked these questions?
*What do you notice about the question/s?
*What do you notice about your response/s?
*Is the art of asking "right" questions something you do, as a
    natural function of your everyday life?
*How can you be more conscious in the participation of the art
    of right questioning?

A "Mystery" Practice: The Act of Asking Right Questions

*Think of a situation that you are involved in or have been involved in, that did not turn out according to what you would have liked to see happen. Make a note of the situation.

When this situation was brought to your attention what type of questions, did you ask of yourself and/or others about the situation? Be honest, did you ask, "Who is to blame? Why did this happen?" "Why is this happening again?" "Why didn't I...?" "Why didn't he/she?" "Whose fault was it, for it wasn't mine?"

Make a note of the questions you remember asking.

If in a group, find a partner, and discuss the situation and your questions, taking two minutes each to share.

Looking at history in order to learn from it, what "right questions" would you ask if confronted with the same situation?

Spiral Dynamics an Integrative Tool for Leadership and Life

*"By exploring and describing the core intelligences
and deep values that flow beneath what we believe and do,
Spiral Dynamics[56] offers a profoundly incisive,
dynamic perspective on complex matters
such as how people think about things
(as opposed to what they think),
why people make decisions in different ways,
and why people respond to different motivators.* [57]
--Don Beck

Spiral Dynamics is a conceptual framework that has the depth and potential for a behavioral impact for those who are willing to dive into the interiors of its belly of wisdom and knowledge. Spiral Dynamics is a sociological, psychological, and historical treatise on the dynamics of human values, human behaviors, historical reflection, and spiritual growth as each has evolved through levels of time and conscious awareness. Describing the levels of consciousness and structures of values a group holds and/or exists in, Spiral Dynamics opens the way for moving past surface issues and delving into the deeper issues that await identification and addressing.

Spiral Dynamics creates a framework for understanding the forces at work in the growth of awareness in human consciousness as impacted by the experiences of the human condition. Each level on the spiral has certain beliefs, social and motivational patterning, and goals. Clare Graves, original

---

[56] Beck, Don and Cowan, Christopher. *Spiral Dynamics.* Blackwell Publishing. Oxford, UK. 1996
[57] Beck, Don and Cowan, Christopher. *Spiral Dynamics.* Blackwell Publishing. Oxford, UK. 1996

researcher and developer of Spiral Dynamics, created a "macro-model" of human consciousness that clarifies the developmental processes of collective groups, organizations, and entire countries. It is said that, "*other conceptual models easily fit inside this very expansive view.*"

Research gleaned from worldwide studies spanning five decades and 50,000 interviews, underpins the idea that cognitive development occurs in stages; Maslow's hierarchy of needs reflects this idea, also. To move from one stage or level to another requires a shift or leap in conscious awareness because each new stage calls forth a fresh set of values to engage with and live from.

Clare Graves on the Spiral

Clare Graves initiated his research on human dynamics in the 1970s. Graves, a sociologist, traced the values and psychology of humankind back to its beginnings. He wanted to study how consciousness has evolved and what it had to teach us about ourselves through this evolvement.

Graves believed that human events move in a spiral manner, coming full circle, at a level above where they started when there is a movement of great transformation afoot.   The spiral is one of the most ancient of symbols. Symbolically, its shape represents the cycles of the journey through "birth-death-rebirth". Thus, the spiral represents the interior journey to Self.

The journey on the spiral is an inherently dynamic movement, as it never takes us back to the same place. Initiating movement on the spiral, always ends with the result of an upward type movement or being at a higher position on the spiral. A spiral is not linear, it is circular and it turns.

As the conditions of human existence shift and change creating new systems, the older systems do not go away, they remain. Human nature is neither static nor finite, it is in constant motion. When paradigm shifts are activated, the rules of living are adapted to work within the context of the new paradigm. This is true for individuals, groups, and businesses.

Graves asserts that when humankind has a leap in consciousness, or comes back around in a full circle turn, they do so at a different level of awareness. Thus, this is why humankind shifts the rules (psychologically and sociologically) to adapt to the arising and new conditions. Let us look at the printing press from this perspective of rules: shifting in order to adapt to new conditions arising.

Prior to the printing press, information to the masses was limited, due to the lack of ability to get information out to the public; and to the fact that often information was withheld from the public by those in positions of authority. It was a subtle way of controlling the masses.

Humankind then was in the dark, so to speak, about what was happening; except for rumors and what those in authority wanted the public to know.

Once the printing press made it possible for information to be available and disseminated, the shift that resulted for human kind was multi-fold. Not only was information available, but the adaptation that resulted was that the masses had a desire and the need to learn to read in order to stay informed. Humankind adapted to the new condition arising.

The impact this concept has for leadership and organizations is that organizations can only respond to the level of current culture and values being expressed within the organization. If the organization's leadership is not an open 'living' system that encourages advancement in management models and motivational concepts, the organization will eventually find that they will be left behind through innovation and re-invention by other groups.

As we begin our journey into the spiral, let us look at the pictorial concept of the spiral as depicted in *Spiral Dynamics*[58]. For now, just take note of the colors and where their level fits on the spiral. A detailed explanation of each level is described on the chart below the picture of the spiral.

A Picture of the Spiral   (Refer to last page of book for picture)
The Evolving Spiral of Human Values and Conditions

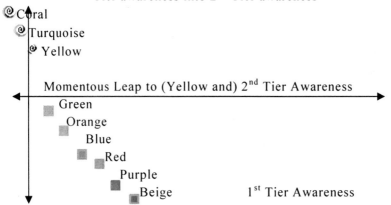

It takes a momentous leap in consciousness to cross from 1st Tier awareness into 2nd Tier awareness

Coral
Turquoise
Yellow

Momentous Leap to (Yellow and) 2nd Tier Awareness

Green
Orange
Blue
Red
Purple
Beige   1st Tier Awareness

Refer to the back cover for a detailed picture of the diagram

Humankind tends to make a leap in consciousness, when collective consciousness embraces a new paradigm of values, then it plateaus for thousands or hundreds of years or lately, every few decades – then it jumps again.

---

58 Beck, Don and Christopher Cowan. *Spiral Dynamics.*

Clare Graves reported that Beige awareness and values (Instinct and Survival) began 250,000 years ago and lasted for nearly 215,000 years; Purple (Magical Thinking and Rituals) came into being at that time, which was about 35,000 years ago. 10,000 years ago Red (Ego Identity) evolved, then we (humankind) moved into Blue (Law and Order), 2,800 years ago. We moved into Orange (Autonomy, Democracy, Scientific Data, Entrepreneurs), awareness only 400 years ago.

Now our leaps in consciousness, and the corresponding values they support, are occurring more frequently. Green (Egalitarian, Environmentalists, Peace-Makers) became apparent about 150 years ago and less than 50 years ago we started the turn into integrative Yellow (Integral, High Principles, Wisdom). Now we are moving into an awareness of what, perhaps, Turquoise holds (BE! NOW- as in present moment, quantum-oriented).

Author, Peter Russell, a decade ago, in his book, *A White Hole in Time,* asked collective humankind the following question; *"Where are we going and where are going so quickly?"* Where will all this knowledge and shift in values take us, as individuals and as an inter-connected group of world citizens?

Although the movement on the 1st tier of the spiral is speeding up, moving into 2nd tier awareness would require a momentous leap in thinking, values, and action. What this leap into 2nd tier awareness entails is just now being unearthed, for as a species we are just starting to gain this knowledge.

Spiral Dynamics [59] co-author Don Beck purports that 10% (1% is 60 million of 6 billion people) of the world's population is at the Green level of awareness and only .01% is at the place of the momentous leap, Yellow. Thus, humankind has a way to go in conscious evolution and growth to begin the movement into Yellow Integrative awareness. Additionally, in 1st tier each level believes that it's values and view of life is the only right and correct one; even Green, which purports to be so inclusive and egalitarian.

As we make reference to the evolving spiral and the growth it brings, please note that no level of the spiral is considered better than another; some may be more effective in bringing about change, but we must grow through, then transcend and include, all levels of the spiral.

[59] Beck, Don and Cowan, Christopher. *Spiral Dynamics.* Blackwell Publishing. Oxford, UK. 1996

A Review of the Levels of the Spiral

Color	*Consciousness Levels, Values, and the Human Condition*

Beige
Survival
.01% of
World's
Population

Healthy Beige:
Is about instinct and survival behaviors and the fight, flight, or flee feelings that arise when we are in danger or in peril.
It is about automatic responses, being on auto-pilot, staying alive, and meeting our biological needs on a daily basis.
Unhealthy Beige:
Survival consumes them and they lack an adequate language or energy capacity for a discussion of the issues.
Does not have the capacity for reflective thinking.
Life's Great Meaning for Beige:
Life has great meaning when I survive another day and when I can reproduce the species.

Purple
Magic
10% of
World's
Population

Healthy Purple:
Initiates reflective thinking.
Uses oral tradition, story-telling, honoring elders, participation in sacred ritual.
Gathers in tribes and is about bonding.
Believes in the magical, is superstitious, and creates ritual to support beliefs and to protect self and others.
Unhealthy Purple:
Magical thinking occurring in inappropriate situations.
e.g., I envision a bubble around me while sitting on a railroad track, believing the bubble will protect me and I will be safe. I over-spend and believe that God will provide all the money I need.
Believes in ritual and ritualistic sacrifice, is fear-filled and superstitious.
NOTE: All tier 1 is fear-filled and/or fear-oriented.
Uses sacrifice (human or other) to appease the gods and/or their gang leaders. (Gangs are purple/red)
Creates tribal, group, and/or ethnic wars to protect "tribe".
Ritual killing (or other harm) is accepted as a rite of passage.
Life's Great Meaning for Purple:
Life has it greatest meaning when I can protect myself and my collected group or tribe.

Red
Power
20% of
World's
Population

Healthy Red:
Ego identity begins the journey apart from the tribe/family.
The individual feels his/her power and wants to impulsively act to satisfy personal wants and needs.
Ego takes deep root, self-identification, power, and conquering in the name of 'ownership'; to be mine.

Me, myself, and I, are very important.
Is competitive (true of Orange also), independent, and can take self-initiated action.
Has courage, are the heroes (heroes are often a Blue/ Red combination)
Takes responsibility for the things they own.

Unhealthy Red:
Rage, consumed by a consciousness of competition, of winning and losing, and using cruelty in the name of competition.
Going to extremes, whether in exercise or work.
Gets very upset when things do not go their way; narcissistic.
Does not like to share their 'stage', power, or wealth.
Warlords and Thugs

Life's Great Meaning for Red:
Life has its greatest meaning when I am recognized for who I am and what I do and have.

Blue Law and Order 40% of World's Population	*Healthy Blue*: Creates rules, policies, procedures, order and dogmas. Are about levels of authority, fundamentalism of any kind, right use of the right rules, and have only one right way to do things and that is their way. Blue came about when red became so violent that rules and laws had to be instituted in order for people to be held accountable for their actions. Gather great strength and meaning from their God. NOTE: People are not just one color, but a combination of colors, as we transcend and include on the spiral. *Unhealthy Blue*: Absolute Law and Order, Authority and Authoritarianism or total dependency on authority to tell them what to do. Feel they must follow the rules and puts order of tradition above moving forward in progress. Extremists, Blues say there is only one true doctrine and it is what I say to be true or believe to be true: from eating your vegetables because they make you strong, to you must believe this doctrine in order to save yourself. Hierarchy, Crusades and Inquisition *Life's Great Meaning for Blue*: Life has it greatest meaning when rules are followed and order is established through policy.
Orange Autonomy 30% of World's Population	*Healthy Orange*: Orange is about autonomy and democracy; they are the scientists, entrepreneurs, achievers, strategists, users of precise language, and opportunists. Orange relies on empirical data, "show me" – verify what you say and I'll show you verification that what I say is true. Honor capitalism and entrepreneurship.

Believe the world is bursting with opportunities.
Orange value values and want goals, they like to set goals and achieve those goals.
Wants rewards for accomplishments and believes they are the best at what they do.
Unhealthy Orange:
Orange will act in own self-interest to achieve goals.
Rational head-centered rather than heart-orientation.
Uses the resources of Mother Earth without regard for future generations.
Life's Great Meaning for Orange:
Life has its greatest meaning when I am making money, proving my theories to be correct or I have reached my goal.
Life is about achievement, challenge, learning, striving to succeed, and making the world better by solving problems with science and technology.

Green
Egalitarian
10% of
World's
Population

Healthy Green:
Willingness to look at self and God in new ways, they are sensitive, introspective, egalitarian, environmentalists, and peace-makers and keepers.
Wants input from everyone, better to continue dialogue than to make a decision that not everyone might agree with, consensus-oriented.
Inclusive.
A holistic healing orientation.
Community oriented, wants to give to all, and desires to increase awareness on all types of issues.
Heart oriented from what they understand to be of the heart, are expressing compassion in their way.
Unhealthy Green:
Tendency to "burn out" from all they do because they *care* so much.
So attached to their views, they are not necessarily good leaders, and can easily return to narcissism and ego-centrism.
Can become the "mean green" when they see only from their perspective.
    e.g., "If you wear fur, I will throw paint on you."
Green is susceptible to "group" think and are extreme in their caring about others and yet are often blind to other levels of consciousness having a right to exist if they are not in alignment with what green believes.
    e.g., Green dislikes and are disgusted by rules of blue, and capitalism of orange, perceived exploitation of natural resources and other types of resources such as money, etc.
Often cannot give room for others to follow traditional routes of medicine, due to their entrenched holistic beliefs. In fact, they will ask an ill person, "What in your consciousness caused this ...?" Think they are advanced in consciousness but often are – Metaphysizlers"

Life's Great Meaning for Green:
My sense of ambition is shifting into a greater understanding of the deeper meaning of life and knowing I can help. When I know that everyone has been included, I am content.

Yellow
Integrative
.01% of
World's
Population

Healthy Yellow:
Yellow is the momentous leap into 2nd tier consciousness. In infancy of yellow and perhaps 2nd Tier shadow still exists.
Yellow is integrative and integral in all it does.
Yellow is integrative of the head and heart, lives from wisdom and compassion and the desire to be of service. Desires to communicate with wisdom and compassion.
Yellow is very self-aware and self- observant, is holistic.
Yellow is comfortable in living and working in the global world and using the technology and tools of the day.
Yellow understands we need the blue of order and the movement of scientific knowledge, and individualists, etc.
Highly principled, self-directed, and has values competence – not necessarily universally competent.
Moving into a simplistic understanding of what it means to live BE.
Yellow is focused on action to solve problems. It is survival echoed at 2nd Tier.
Working to make a difference.
Fears are recognized and no long controls life. Although the role of the ego is understood, this doesn't mean
Yellow has full management of the ego.
Has capacity to recognize 'toxicity' of each level and help to shift and/or release the unhealthy aspects.
Ambition is integrated into a greater meaning for life.
Yellow is still head-centered somewhat – head with heart.
Some say that Yellow claims a higher wisdom than it actually has.
Unhealthy Yellow:
Could become too self-reliant or self-contained (not as in being an introvert), as in needs no one else, however, they would be conscious enough to recognize that this is happening and would do so within a very short time frame.
People can be cognitively Yellow and still be jerks because of other "lines" or levels trailing. Yellow is not to be idealized.
Life's Great Meaning for Yellow:
When making a difference. When Yellow is fully functional it crosses all levels (it has "vertical awareness") and begins to evolve Turquoise.

Turquoise 2nd Tier *BE*	*Healthy Turquoise*: Turquoise lives *BE*, is whole oriented and is in the energetic flow of life. Is a mediator, utilizing discernment and judgment; discernment comes through connection with a higher wisdom. Turquoise understands that what happens in one place affects all and is the whole 'living' system oriented vs. the parts. Diversity rules. Lives from gnosis-cardia, the head has given permission to the heart to live from heart wisdom. Turquoise lives compassion, in balance. Lives and serves in life for the greater meaning rather than money or adulation. Turquoise senses no difference in living a spiritual life and living life for spirit pervades all and makes everything a sacred act. Turquoise aligns with the moment and things happen quickly, as in almost a no space/time continuum. Turquoise has no fear, for they understand there is only One Presence and it is Good and all it created was called Good. Turquoise is about wholeness and achieving a true balance in connection with a higher source of self. In calling for the wholeness of a person, it has the capacity to shift a whole community, country, and/or organization. Turquoise are not insular, they are changeable, flexible, and grounded in wisdom and discernment. Turquoise has transcended, "me alone" and integrated a "us" cooperative consciousness. Lives from a conscious awareness of self-observation and understanding that by connecting to the energy of the moment, they can look past appearances and "see" what is arising out of the content of the chaos or energy in the moment. Feels a connection to all sentient beings. Understands the energetic unified-field and what it means to BE in resonance with a person, situation, and/or organization. Thinks in 'Big' picture, beyond appearances. *Unhealthy Turquoise*: At this level, the person would *BE* in a state of continual conscious awareness and thus, *BE* fully aware when unhealthy or chaotic tendencies arise and they would have the capacity to shift consciousness quickly to support a realignment of energy. *Life's Great Meaning*: Comes from the act of service, serving in wisdom and compassion, and from having healthy communication with all levels. *BE*! In every moment, *BE* Principle in action-the personal ego is dissolving into impersonal.
Coral 2nd Tier	*Healthy Coral*: Coral is listed and as with Turquoise, the attributes of Coral are just beginning to unfold and be recognized. According to Graves, Coral, understands 1st tier levels and may even be

having or experiencing the same issues as in 1st tier but has a deeper understanding, compassion, and energetic where-with-all to move through them very quickly.

Spiral Leadership Styles

Because humankind, as a collective whole, does not experience the same life conditions or hold the same worldviews, it would seem appropriate to say that we do not all lead in the same manner. If differing views bring on differing ideas about what is important to an individual, it would seem logical that this would spill over into leadership styles. Clare Graves said that people are in error when:

> *"They assume the nature of man (humankind) is fixed*
> *and there is a single set of human values*
> *by which he/she should live".*

Let us say that by virtue of the nature of humankind, there are not fixed or static values. If values differ, then leadership and management skills will differ greatly based upon what the person values most on the spiral.

e.g., If a person grew up within a family system that values rules and order, then rules will be instituted within their organizational system and they will make sure that people follow them.

The following is an overview of the leadership qualities that each level of the spiral holds for that value system. It reflects what they value as a worker and/or leader. The spiral is not a jump from one level another, there is an overlaying or, blending effect that occurs, such as red to blue, blue to orange awareness, etc. Thus, one does not wake up one day and say, "now Green awareness has been established over all levels of my life."

A "Mystery" Practice: My Spiral Leadership Style

> *"The leaders' values define the culture of an organization,*
> *and the culture defines the organizations*
> *competitive advantage or level of mission assurance."* [60]
> Richard Barrett

In reviewing the chart, notice and then be interested in your personal leadership style. Even if you do not have a title that says manager, director, supervisor– you still have a leadership style that you put into place in your everyday life. Notice what traits you see in yourself, and then include others with whom you interact within your organization. Additionally, take notice of

---

[60] Barrett, Richard. *Liberating the Corporate Soul.* Butterworth-Heinemann. San Francisco, CA. 1998

what, if anything, interests you about the various leadership qualities and why? Note: You may have more than one level reflected in your style.

Spiral Leadership Styles

Color	Spiral Levels and Values Reflect Leadership Styles and Qualities
Beige	*Leadership Styles and Qualities: Instinctual Responders*
Torbert-Action Logic Name (TALN) Instinctual	*Healthy-Positive Leadership Qualities:* Beige is about automatic and instinctual responses, thus, one would not normally be in Beige awareness for a long periods of time. Instinctual survival skills may kick-in for short-periods of time, however, they are "managed" by purple and blue rules. As a healthy instinct response, there could be an instantaneous prioritization according to the seriousness of the situation. These are automatic and instinctual responses. *Unhealthy*: View the work environment from the filter of – Can this harm me? How can I protect myself? Fear and the need for self-survival leads them; thus they stick with what they know and develop work-preserving habits. Are on auto-pilot. Use the elements of fight, flight, or freeze when confronted with issues, problems, situations, and often in interaction with personnel; or people in general. Reactive by nature, can create crisis. Question: "Is there a crisis or do they turn situations into a crisis?"
Purple	*Leadership Styles and Qualities: Mother-Father Figure*
(TALN) Impulsive	*Healthy-Positive Leadership Qualities:* Benevolent, caring as parent figure, often generous, acts as a Mother or Father to group, has a strength that can be counted on strong, believes they act for the good of the "family": without consulting the family. Creates myths and traditions for the organization such as, birthday celebrations, outings, yearly party to honor parental figure, etc. Helps to fosters sense of "family" within group, are loyal, and may sacrifice their needs to be part of group and receive protection from group. *Unhealthy*: Knows what is good for the whole organization; without consulting the whole organization or any one person besides their self. May stay too long in leadership because they are the founder

and thus, doesn't move the company forward. Things are good the way they are, why take a chance and ruin them.

Sticks together in the confines of the "tribe".

Gives allegiance to those who hold the responsibility for the work-wellbeing.

Treats employees like they are their children and wants the children to run to them with problems; this reinforces how much they are needed.

Sense of family often taps into dysfunctional family dynamics.

We are a tribe and no one messes with or enters the tribe without invitation.

Benevolent dictator, advises and protect while negating individual choice.

Red

(TALN)
Opportunist

Leadership Styles and Qualities: Power-full Authoritarian Manager

Healthy-Positive Leadership Qualities:

Able to assert a sense of self; has the ability to let others see their strength.

Has a sense of authority; doesn't back down; don't constrain me.

Feels sense of responsibility.

Courageous, risk-taker, will speak up and stand up when needed.

Acts spontaneously and impulsively; with little or no guilt.

Always on alert for possible dangers.

Creative.

Unhealthy:

The leader behaves with aggression and try's to solve problems in the same manner. Dominator.

Wants instant gratification for their demands; which often means moving projects around with lack of concern for consequences.

The leader demands loyalty without question; is controlling.

Narcissistic and may be prone to rage.

Large sense of self as boss; due to inflated ego.

Intimidation and might are greater than discussion.

Power held over people.

Blue

(TALN)
Diplomat→
Expert
(B/O)

Leadership Styles and Qualities: Law and Order Manager

Healthy-Positive Leadership Qualities:

As leader has a detailed organizational structure, with clear lines of authority.

Brings organization to chaos.

Roles for all involved are clearly delineated.

Has a defined set of rules, rewards, and punishments in place for actions – goes by the book.

As a leader likes order and reflects stability.

Discipline is seen as positive.

Has the desire to understand meaning and purpose of life and of a higher power.

Will sacrifice right now for rewards that will come later.

Self-disciplined and believes that loyalty brings advancement.

Unhealthy:

Fascist, extremist, there is a loss of individual freedom due to absolutism of rules.

Need for extreme control and often controls through guilt.

Everyone has their place and so, don't step beyond your bounds.

Orange   *Leadership Styles and Qualities:*   *Autonomy Manager*

(TALN)

Expert →

Achiever

Healthy-Positive Leadership Qualities:

Assertive, entrepreneurial, competitive, likes to drive change, but not necessarily to have change done to itself.

Wants data to support research, and research to support direction; give me the numbers that support the research.

Optimistic, a strategist, goal oriented.

Wants economic compensation commensurate with effort.

Wants scientific truths and science to prove the truths; progress is a result of discovery; and measures need to be in place to measure the progress.

A networker, technology and materially oriented.

About equality and justice.

Unhealthy:

Unless data proves it, I won't believe it or participate – may not be totally unhealthy.

I learn so I can be smarter than my competition, an opportunist.

Materialistic to the point of major excess.

Destroys the environment through the overuse of resources.

Will sacrifice resources (human and other-wise) to make money.

Green   *Leadership Styles and Qualities: Humanitarian Leader*

(TALN)

Individualist

Healthy-Positive Leadership Qualities:

Works diligently to achieve consensus so everyone feels good about the decision.

Learning to respond vs. react; and conflict needs to be avoided.

Practicing higher principles, and personal and spiritual growth.

Involved in humanitarian efforts.

Seeks harmony, through acceptance, belonging, diversity.

Seeks to understand the inner nature and the interior life.

Caring wants to be seen as helper/friend more than manager. Community builders.

Desires to model and lead, not manage – works most of the time.

Seeking ideologies that enhance self-growth and awareness.

Unhealthy:

So oriented towards consensus things may not get done. May be ineffective as leaders due to need to for all to get along.

Resists hierarchy, authority, and may not do well in established, traditional work environments.

Too caring tend to burnout.

Has no room for styles or values other than own, disrespects hierarchy and rules, etc.

Yellow—Integrative

(TALN) Strategist

Leadership Styles and Qualities: Integrative Leadership

Healthy-Positive Leadership Qualities:

Integrative style of management and utilizes whole "living" systems approach.

Knows that chaos is inherent in order and to move through change.

Learns for own sake (self-directed) thus, is cognizant of world issues and prepares for their impact.

Always looking for a way to integrate people, projects, etc.

Believes in Accountability vs. Responsibility

Vision and Mission clear and aligned with a greater purpose. Integrates wisdom, passion, and compassion.

Knows they need all levels for creative unity and purpose fulfillment and can work from a healthy integrative perspective with all levels.

Makes choices based on appropriateness of conditions; doesn't fear outside forces' impact on organization, but is aware of what they are.

Models and manages, and leads; yellow is a both/and.

Knows when to coach, when to challenge, when to supervise, and when to inspire.

Practices both a coaching and a managerial model.

Practices interior listening and other ideologies that enhance self-growth and awareness.

Aware of and utilizes multiple teachings for organizational development.

Original in thinking.

Work and life are in unity. A big picture person.

Unhealthy:

Moving into 2nd tier unhealthy values are recognized and then consciously integrated. If remnants of 1st tier unhealthy values arise this leader will be aware of them and adjust their approaches and behaviors accordingly.

Turquoise 2nd Tier	Leadership Styles and Qualities: BE (and Invites Others to BE)
(TALN) Alchemist→ Ironist	*Healthy-Positive Leadership Qualities:* Works from a global standpoint and interest. Utilizes multi-disciplinary approaches, understands regardless of appearance "it's all small stuff". Compassionate, open, transparent and shares information. Principled, with clear core values; leads from an innate, intuitive wisdom. Stands in awe of cosmic order. Is humble, self-integrated, holistic, intuitive, and lives interior listening. Is conscious and aware of energy arising in situation, self, and in world. Energetically in tune with self and others and sees connection of spirit and self. Lives the –Q- 'living' systems model and understands evolutionary flow. Creates space for flex-flow in the system(flexibility and flow). Is dynamic and that dynamism arises in relationship to what is happening around them. Aware of and utilizes multiple teachings for organizational development. Lives from a sense of freedom and has no fear, is calm and poised, not staged. Lives and is principle expressing. Original in thinking. Understands the nuance and important of *BE*-ing in the question. Lives non-resistance, non-attachment, and non-judgment. Lives compassion in action and grace, lives simplicity. *Unhealthy*: Don't know the full impact of this, as of yet, however, when moving into 2nd tier unhealthy qualities will likely be small remnants left from other levels that still require honing. This leader will be aware of their behaviors and adjust them based on what they see is arising in the field in which they are participating.
Coral 2nd Tier	***Leadership Styles and Qualities: IS***
(TALN) Ironist	*Healthy-Positive Leadership Qualities:* Has integrated all of the values previously mentioned and is evolving into new values that are not yet understood or revealed in consciousness.

On becoming a leader:
"Lead yourself first with such authenticity
and depth that other people will choose to follow"
-- Cindy Wigglesworth,
Spiritual Intelligence

Please note that whether you are a small or large business, a church or school board, etc., you will want persons from every value-set or turn on the spiral involved in whatever type work you are doing. Here is how each (healthy) level can assist within the group or organization:

Orange (Marketing/CEO/COO/IT/etc.) will assist in keeping the group on a cutting edge of enterprise and economically on track. Blue (Accounting/CFO/etc.) will help assure that order prevails and rules are followed as defined; will want to know best practices and adhere to them vehemently. Green (Human Resources/etc.) holds compassion for all and the space for all to participate and to be heard. Purple is benevolent and holds tradition. Beige often works well in crisis. Red is very creative and expressive and can be of tremendous value when their ego is in check. Yellow (CEO/COO/etc.) provides stability, accountability, and models best practices. Those with Turquoise leanings make wonder-filled leaders and employees/share-holders. All of the positions listed above are given in the name of possibility, only. Anyone within an organization can hold these value systems and express them in their daily work environment.

The differences between Green, Yellow, Turquoise, and Coral with their regard for a capacity of self-growth and awareness is:

Green seeks and practices self-growth values (to the degree that they do not interfere with their strongly held beliefs);

Yellow integrates the values;

Turquoise will live the values and truths associated with the values.

Coral IS – and has all the values integrated in every fiber of their being.

The true gift of 2nd tier spiral leadership is that they have transcended and included each level of the spiral, thus, they are aware of the healthy and unhealthy aspects of all levels. Thus, they see what is good, true, and beautiful about each of the previous levels and they know how each level deals (appropriately and effectively) with certain life conditions and can tap into that wisdom. Additionally, they understand the limitations of each level and when it goes toxic, can set appropriate boundaries.

2nd Tier leaders also, have the capacity to honor and respect what others value, without having to agree with them. When we can honor the values of others, without making them feel small or unheard, we open the way for dynamic dialogue that creates connection across all levels.

"By looking at the formation of structures in the past,
using empirical and historical research...
we can focus our attention on that (old) leading edge of evolution
and help a new leading edge of evolution to move forward."
--Ken Wilbur

Coherence and Incoherence in Organizational Systems:

It has been said that trust and openness are two components found in organizations that are coherent in nature. What else constitutes a coherent organization?

When an organization is in coherence, the actions and outcomes of the system are aligned with who the organization says they are; and we discover who an organization is, through their vision, mission, and core values.

A corporate vision statement shares with the world, who the organization says they are in the world. It is the company's biggest dream or vision about being in service to the world and the population they serve; it is why they exist. A mission is how the organization puts their biggest dream into action in the world. Both are usually, short, concise, simple, and yet highly effective statements of being and action. Core values are the talk the organization walks. Core values reflect what the organization stands for in the world and what they model; not what they say they model.

One company I worked with came up with the following core values; innovation, imagination, inspiration. What this means is that when a person interacted with that organization (and the organization was in coherence within all of its systems); the person could expect that all their interactions and outcomes from that interaction, would reflect these three core values. The interactions would be innovative, imaginative, and inspirational. When an organization or a person is in coherence, they do what they said they would do, in a way that is aligned with who they say they are, through their core values. All of these principles working together create success in interactions.

Coherence is also reflected within a company when a feeling of satisfaction and all is well, permeates the work arena. The "employees"-"co-workers"-"stake-holders" feel fulfilled in what they do; their work gives them a sense of meaning; and there is an underlying feeling of harmony that infuses the system. These arise because the organization and its co-workers are demonstrating as a collective whole, externally and internally, who they say they are.

We also can recognize when an organization is not in coherence, or is in incoherence. Incoherence occurs when the actions and outcomes of an organization not in alignment with who the organization says they are; as purported through their vision, mission, and core values. Incoherence is easy to detect because of its symptoms.

The first symptom is one of energy – either a negative energy tone is prevalent, such as dissatisfaction, or a lack of energy is felt within the system. Energy can be felt and energy does not lie.

Regardless of which one it is, negative energy or lack of energy; energetically both are palpable to the people who come into the system, either to work or to do business.

Negative undertones create a palpable energy that exists within the system and affects all those who enter the system even for a short while. This undercurrent of negative energy will eventually give rise to and be reflected throughout the organization as escalating feelings of *"frustration, resignation, and a sense of cynicism"*. These symptoms develop in the order presented, and continue to escalate if not addressed. These symptoms are addressed by becoming aware of the energy currently arising within the system and taking authentic actions to shift them.

As with people, organizations can also go unconscious. They can ignore what is happening before their very eyes; they refuse to see or feel the energy emanating from within the boundaries of the organizational system. So, how does an organization get conscious again? Consciousness is restored *through honest self-observation and self-evaluation.* Sometimes it takes an unbiased person from outside the organization to assist in this process.

Let us now look at another positive-solution model for the creation of extraordinary experiences within the work environment.

Extraordinary Transformational Experiences (ETE)

> *"Until one is able to be honest with their thoughts, feelings,*
> *and responses; authenticity is veiled."* [61]
> **--TGB**

Imagine a company where the people in the organization create an intention for and then commit to experiencing extraordinary transformational experiences (ETE), as part of their daily work practices!

What is an extraordinary transformational experience? An ETE is an experience in which the ordinary is changed into the extra-ordinary and even possibly, the extraordinary.

Extraordinary experiences are per, former National Geographical photographer, Dewitt Jones:

> *"...experiences that are very unusual and deserving attention and comment because of being wonderful, excellent ... and as going beyond the scope of something in ... established use".* [62]

---

[61] Boehm, Toni G. The Spiritual Intrapreneur. Inner Visioning Press. Greenwood. MO.

To *transform* means to change, shift, convert, create something new out of the old, change markedly the form or appearance, change the nature of, or to subject a person, situation, or condition to the action of a transformer – as in electricity or Spirit.

Experience is the apprehension of an object, thought, or emotion through the senses or mind; active participation in events or activities leading to the accumulation of knowledge or skills; to participate in or partake of personally; or an event or series of events participated in or lived through.

ETE's occur when there is an active participation in an event or conversation, which takes the group beyond the everyday mundane into an elevated awareness that holds the space for the moment to be appreciative, new, wonderful, excellent, transformative, and potentially life changing. Thus, it is important as part of everyday life to begin to create an expectation or mind-set for the occurrence of ETE's.

Setting the Intention for an ETE to Occur

Intentions are vehicles that transform universal energy into a "power" that can infuse our thoughts and actions. Intentions determine what is possible for our lives. The manifestation of our intention/s is intertwined with our belief system and our perceptions. To determine how our intentions will manifest, let us look at our beliefs and their influencer – our perceptions or thought-filters.

Beliefs are a collection of perceptions that have in a sense concretized. Perceptions are the filters through which we see reality; they based upon the beliefs we hold. It is a circular type of existence; beliefs create the thought-filters for perception and perceptions create the basis of beliefs. One influences and impacts the other and it just keeps going around until we make a conscious choice to change our beliefs. Conscious choices are upheld and supported through the creation of intentions, the words and actions that we use to transform energy and call forth success.

Take a moment to consider and create an intention for yourself and/or team that would open the door to extraordinary transformational experiences and conversations in your work environment and/or your personal life.

ETE Intention:

I intend to create extraordinary transformational experiences in my life, to do this I will- _____ -and I will start this by- ___ (date).

Jones, Dewitt. Star Productions. Video.

Creating Extraordinary Transforming Conversations

Although the opportunities in life are limitless, an avenue for the creation of ETEs is through our conversations. Conversation is defined as; a vehicle of communication that takes place between two or more persons. An extraordinary transforming communication experience or conversation would be a dialogue between two or more persons that has the potential to go beyond the ordinary exchange of words into a deep, appreciative, and profound life changing experience.

We can consciously support and create intentions for extraordinary transforming conversations through active engagement in conversations in the following ways:

- Consciously choose to make each conversation a transforming one thru generous listening
- Be a generous listener, wait for others to finish their thought before jumping in to share yours.
- Focus on what the other person is saying, not on what you want to say next.
- Give the other person your full attention.
- When practicing interior listening keep your attention focused in your heart
- Participate in honest and authentic dialogue, with yourself and others.

Honest, authentic dialogue is open and truthful; it does not have to have embellishments or untruths added, in order to make one's self look good. Authentic dialogue allows for revelation of self without feeling silly, embarrassed, a need to hide something, or keeping secrets. (Secrets are toxic to our physical, mental, and emotional well-being, as well as to the depth of true intimacy we can attain in our relationships.)

When we risk being vulnerable and truthful there is an opportunity for a shift in understanding to occur. Being vulnerable means that we are willing to risk exposure, but we can only do this when we are not attached any longer to our toxic secrets and their unhealed emotional components.

When we utilize and model positive-focused questioning and decision-making processes and communicate focusing on positive-oriented results, a shift occurs in our conversations just from having held those ideals as our intention.

However, please note, that this does not mean that we are to sugar-coat everything we say, so that we will not create any disturbances in our conversations – no – chaos often calls forth clarity, so do not fear or distain its presence.

Wrap-Up: -Q-, the Evolutionary Pulse, and the Work Place

Humanity is evolving at a rapid rate and the previously mentioned quantum values are fast becoming the leading edge of emerging values within humanity and thus, will roll over into and change leadership styles and values. Please note, that this is not about good or bad or either/or, regarding the Newtonian and -Q- Living Systems paradigm differences. It is about the impact of the differences and where the growing-edges of new awareness are taking humankind.

As a result of this fresh edge of growth, we are looking to see how leadership values are being affected and how the AQAL Chart of the individual-collective-internal-external might be effected.

e.g., One major value currently shifting is the way people are valuing their personal life; most do not want a five and six-day work week. They want to work faster and smarter. Additionally, employees want freedom; the freedom to work from their homes, without being tethered to a go-to office. People are looking to find a balance between their values and their need for employment. This one value-shift will have great impact on the work environment as it continues to evolve in the consciousness awareness of humankind.

You cannot have new emerging values and not have them impact the totality of all of the portions of human life in general – the AQAL. Even though by outer appearances it looks as if greed is still the strong corporate and individual motivator, ideology is shifting; and it will be reflected in all aspects of life in the next 20 to 25 years or sooner.

It appears that a new paradigm is emerging in response to hectic, chaotic life conditions colliding with the values and mores of a desire for interior balance. This desire is creating a shift in our current values systems and we are in the midst of discovering how to live this new shift and its values; not only in the work environment but in all aspects of everyday life

Chapter 6
BE! Building Blocks

> *"Mankind at large always resembles frivolous children;*
> *they are impatient of thought, and wish to be amused.*
> *Truth is too simple for us;*
> *we do not like those who unmask our illusions."*[63]
> --Ralph Waldo Emerson

21ˢᵗ-Century Consciousness:

> *"If you don't realize the S̲ource,*
> *you stumble in the confusion and sorrow.*
> *When you realize where you come from,*
> *you naturally become tolerant,*
> *disengaged, amused, kindhearted... dignified...*
> *immersed in the wonder of the Tao[and]*
> *you can deal with whatever life brings you..."*[64]
> --Tao Te Ching

As we look to the future growth of conscious for humanity and to what the evolution of that growth is revealing, what becomes apparent is that the tool for the 21ˢᵗ century is consciousness. The key to unlocking the toolbox of consciousness, is living from a consciousness aligned with the –Q- field and that of *BE*. *We BE* the energetic state of awareness that we want to see revealed in life.

Over the past several years, as a personal conscious choice, I chose to notice and be more interested in the energy arising in the moment, and what it wanted to reveal to me rather than in the drama that often surrounded it. In doing this, I realized that now is the time to consciously work and align with the –Q- field and to *BE* – not next month or in a year or when I know more – but now!

Make the choice to *BE* – *BE* peace, *BE* interested, *BE* present to life's energies, *BE* love, *BE* joy, *BE* the meditative flow, *BE*. *BE* present to life. Stop participating in excuse making, stop seeking as a means to continue seeking or to find some supposed end, stop practicing the same thing repeatedly, stop creating more opposites in the name of finding Oneness – and "*BE* the change you want to see in the world". *BE* is a stage or level of conscious awareness, that is subtle, tangible, and very real.

---

[63] Emerson, Ralph Waldo. *The Gospel of Emerson.* pg. 90
[64] Lao-Tze. *Tao Te Ching.* Chapter 16

This knowledge of the –Q- field and the power of BE are "living" realities to me, not just words I kibitz about. "Living" realities – it all began – or did it? – as I was preparing dinner in the kitchen. I was walking towards the sink, when I made a conscious choice to turn around and go back into the "keeping room" next to the kitchen – why, I made this choice I cannot remember.

In that one moment, that single, solitary, moment in time – as I turned to shift directions (note, the metaphor), in the midst of the shift – I had an epiphany, a cosmic moment, a cosmic interlude, an experience of the reality of the infinite –Q- field, of *One with all that IS* – an all encompassing, life changing, soul-stirring epiphany[65].

In one tiny moment, the order of the cosmos was revealed and all the "stuff" that had previously seemed so important, was erased or released. In that moment, Toni/self left and what remained was a transparency, for Universal Energy – Love, Peace, Joy, Life – to flow through unimpeded. All was "contained" within the unified field of energy of a higher vibrational frequency, and the field was energetically palpable.

Only *One*, there was no separation, "*I*" was *IT* and *IT* was "*I*" – there was no "me" as in Toni, there was only "*I*"/*One*. The vibration experienced in that moment, the clarity of understanding experienced, changed this mind-body vehicle. The simplicity was overwhelming, I had been consciously, on this journey, for nearly 40 years, and "It" was right here all the time.

Life is not personal, it is impersonal, and is based on natural laws that are always working. Through our choices we are aligned with the laws and principles or we are not. It is from this alignment (or not) that we create our experiences and manifest our intentions (or not).

Our experiences provide contrast in the form of pain or joy. How we respond – in love or fear – to the activity of that contrast, as revealed through our experiences, writes the script of our life. The Universe provides a spiritual feedback mechanism that allows us to identify our beliefs and then to begin to shift and transform those beliefs through freewill. Clarity and simplicity, it was all clear and simple; the journey is about the soul's purpose. The soul's purpose is about soul-growth and a return to unity – and is the reason we said, "yes" to coming to this planet in the first place. Learn to *BE!*

Jesus after his wilderness experience, met his adverse-self again, and the adverse-self (devil) tried to tempt him with riches and power. Jesus said to his adverse-self, "get thee behind me". The adverse-self exists because we are ignorant (not clear) of who we are (BE). The "devil" is a

---

[65] *Encarta Dictionary.* Epiphany: Sudden realization – a sudden intuitive leap of understanding, especially through an ordinary but striking occurrence

cheater and tries to cheat us out of our birthright – of all is Good, and so are we. God-IS – I Am. Know what is false and you will know what it true.

Trying to become, (spiritual, happy, virtuous, etc.) leads to frustration and reinforces the realm of opposites. Good and evil grow on the same tree – our subconscious and conscious minds – and it has no foundation in Truth. Truth is not created in mind, Truth IS and lives in the NOW moment.

What is in mind is a made up idea or version of what we think Truth IS. The only way to freedom – "know the Truth and the Truth will set you free" – is to reveal how one is bound in and by mind, through understanding and facing the cause of conflict, not trying to escape it or sugarcoat it. Understanding frees the mind to be the transparency that experiences the creative power behind all creation.

It was all so transparent – clear and simple – *BE*. That experience led to the writing of this book. Although a novice in many ways, to the full power of the higher –Q- field vibrational frequencies and energy, I know that *BE* is a level of conscious awareness that is subtle, tangible, attainable, and very real. It is my daily "prayer" that this awareness continues to guide my every step and continues to open my consciousness to deeper understandings of what it means to *BE* a 21st century conscious energetic *BE*-ing.

> *"The more 'consciously aware' you become*
> *of how your soul creates –*
> *the higher your frequency goes*
> *and the faster your soul manifests.*
> *Each day your life will become filled with*
> *meaningful coincidences - synchronicities –*
> *that you have attracted –*
> *or created in the grid of*
> *your experiences in the physical."*

Spiritual teachers have purported for centuries that we are individualized expressions of Source, born with a soul that connects us to that Source. Through that the act of being born into life we are introduced to experiences; some good and some painful. Each experience creates an impression that we carry in mind, as thought-energy. As our thought-energy gathers, based upon the types of experiences we have, we create perceptions of what this world is "really" like or about – and it is usually fear-based.

This fear – fear of sickness, fear of "not enough", fear of not being enough, fear of not getting my share, fear of not getting my due, fear of not marrying the right person, fear of not looking good, ... – this fear creates a trance-like state and entrenches us in its reality. Fear (in whatever form it takes) squeezes us as it creates more and more discomfort in our lives. Then one day, often through a power not of our making (per se`) we awaken and we begin the journey back to true self and _S_elf/_S_ource.

We awaken to an understanding or even just a glimpse, of our true nature; but this is often enough, for from this point on we choose to make new choices. We begin the journey of transformation, from believing we are powerless, in a often miserable-type environment or existence, to a person who realizes that through their thoughts they can co-create a new world and experience the joy of living in and as peace and love – free.

We start the journey into the awareness that we are free – free from negativity, free from the need to judge others, free from attachments that have held us in circumstances that perhaps have not been the highest and best, free .... Through practice and application of truth principles, one affirmation at a time, we raise the vibrational frequency flowing through us, from that of a lower, negative-type frequency, to a higher expression – this is what evolution is about.

Evolution of awareness is about the raising of our minds, vibrations, thoughts, feelings, awareness's, energy, etc., into higher levels or dimensions of consciousness that hold more potential, possibility, and capacity for understanding and growth; it is an ever-progressive, upward movement and cycle of learning and expression of that learning. It is a spiritual feedback mechanism that works.

There are teachers creating and modeling 21st century-type curriculums. Curriculums that delve into the depths of how to create the consciousness that supports the conscious awareness of _BE_ in the world. Their curriculum topics and ideas have both juice and depth and are catalysts for expanding into 21st century consciousness, creative partnerships, and quantum transformation.

Every teacher and their curriculum, although different in context and content, has a similar underlying fundamental message. The constant message, even if it is not said this succinctly, is that we are to consciously engage, model, and _BE_ the presence of the energy of non-attachment, non-judgment, non-resistance, non-reaction, peace, Unconditioned Love. _BE_ the presence of this energy in the midst of our life experiences.

Having participated in the personal experience with –Q-, or _S_ource-Energy, and then having studied with various teachers, worked with their curriculums, and having grown through the ensuing experiences, what has been called forth as a result of those interactions (see Spiritual Warrior experience), and what has evolved for me is a collection of 21st century teachings, ideas, and thought-stratagems I refer to as _BE! Building Blocks_ (BBBs).

BBBs are catalysts for spiritual en'lighten'ment and stratagems on how to move into the awareness and consciousness of _BE_. _BBBs_ are tools for the development of conscious awareness. They are intentional, purpose-filled, and create openings in consciousness when utilized in alignment with creative principles and laws (see Chapter 4, on intentions and creating in alignment with universal principles and laws).

As we look to the future growth of consciousness for humanity and to what can be created now in order to assure the evolution of that growth; what becomes apparent is that the tool for the 21st century is consciousness and the key to unlocking the contents of the toolbox is the activity of *BE*, conscious *BE-ing*.

The power or BE! arises in consciousness from continual engagement with the –Q- field and integration of the *BE! Building Blocks*; until one day, we wake up and we *BE* that which we have consciously been integrating! Does this interest you?

Engaging BE! Building Blocks

Before the earth was formed the entire universe was filled with the *"building blocks of matter";* potential, unformed; these "building blocks of matter" were, and continue to be, made up of energy, known as substance. This energy in potential underlies creation and is the energetic substance upon which we imprint our thoughts when we desire to set an intention, create something new, or bring a dream into reality – this energy is what has been referred to as the -Q- field and the imprinting as, conscious –Q- creation. We cannot see this energy or substance, for it is invisible to the naked eye, but do not be deluded, we are imprinting upon it all the time through the action of the dominate thoughts we hold in mind.

The BE! Building Blocks (BBBs) spoken of in this chapter are mind-expanding energetic thought-stratagems (ideas) and are connected to higher-level streams of consciousness. As energetic information, they have an inherent vibration that holds an innate capacity to shift awareness – depending upon how <u>we choose</u> to interact with them.

Conscious, continual, and committed interaction with the   BBBs, has an innate capacity to develop, shift, and expand our thoughts, behaviors, attitudes, beliefs, and/or ideas, through raising and deepening our -Q-vibrational energetic frequencies and levels.

Consciously participating with *BE! Building Blocks* creates shifts within our consciousness and we find that we have grown in awareness just for having consciously interacted with their energy and content. *BBBs* include but are not limited to the thought-stratagems and ideas contained on the following chart. As you read and contemplate these *BBBs*, notice what they stir within you.

It does not matter if every nuance that the words suggest, portray, contain, or represent are understood – if the words create a resonant feeling –

start working with them. The resonant feeling is a confirmation that we are ready to participate.

As the *BBBs* are worked with, and after a time of ripening, there will be a growth in the awareness around who we *BE!* and how we *BE!* In order to be present to life energies, which are only available in the present moment, we must be awake. To be awake we must make the choice to be conscious. When we are conscious we *BE!* the state of awareness and transparency needed for the highest energy stream to create, and manifest the highest good for all.

BE! Building Blocks Chart

In the *BE! Building Blocks Chart* the first block contains an overview of the entire curriculum and is entitled:

BE! Building Block: Seven Principles for Conscious "Living"

Each building block contains information about what is energetically required of us from the perspective of conscious awareness.

BE! Building Blocks
Seven Principles for Conscious "Living"
(Short Version)

1) *BE Intentional* – be "yes", be creativity, be open and   receptive, and ask for what you want

2) *BE Authentic* – be honest, speak your truth, take authentic action and hurt not others

3) *BE Conscious* – be present, be interested, be focused, and be energetically attentive to the –Q- field

4) *BE Aligned* – pray, be *non- attached* to the *things* of the world, be non-resistant, and be the –Q- field

5) *BE Impeccable* – be impeccable in your word, deed, actions, and agreements

6) *BE Accountable* – take responsibility for your experiences and actions

7) *BE!* – it is not about what I do, but who I *BE* as I do it! *BE* Now!

BE! Building Blocks
Seven Principles for Conscious "Living"
(Long Version)

1. BE Intentional: BE "YES!" in conscious action

I know that "YES!" is the creative energy of the universe[66] and the universe is always saying "YES!" to what I hold as a primary thought, intention, and conviction. The universe pulses with "YES!" energies, it does not have a "No" pulse, only "YES!"

I am a conscious _Q_ creator. I know that the universe desires only the highest and best for all involved and that includes me! The universe operates on basic, simple principles and laws. I set intentions and work with those intentions, in alignment with the universal _Q_ principles and laws.

I am conscious that there is a spiritual feedback mechanism or loop that is informing me at all times if I am expressing from the level of love or fear.

Joy informs me when life is sweet. When it is time to grow, I recognize that pain and suffering are the soul's mechanism to alert me that there is "work" to do, root beliefs to shift and transform.

Life is not always "fair". Understanding this I can honestly look at what is literally and energetically happening around and within me; then by remembering and responding from my wholeness, and making new choices, I can move forward in life and consciousness.

It is not what happens to me, but what I choose to do about it, how I choose to respond to it, that ultimately matters!

2. BE Authentic:

"*Conscious BE-ing Leads to Authentic Doing!*"[67] I affirm that my "*conscious being leads to authentic doing*!"   I am authentic when what I do, resonates with who I say I *BE*! If I say I *BE* compassion and then treat others harshly, I am out of alignment with Principle or Law.

---

[66]   Boehm, Toni G. *The Power of YES!*. Inner Visioning Press. Greenwood, MO. 2006
[67]   Simmons, Gary. *I of the Storm*. Unity House. Unity Village, MO. 2001.

Law always acts in alignment with the -Q- field and rewards with equal treatment.

Authenticity supports and leads to right action. When I am asked, "Did you do it?" The only right response or answer is "Yes" or "No". Either I did or I didn't do it. Any other answer is a need to justify my actions and/or to be right and seen as good or perfect.   I do not make excuses for my actions or behaviors. I am accountable and act in accordance.

Success is defined as, "Doing what I said I would do".[68] Did I do what I said I would do? Yes, I did! No, I did not!

3.   *BE Conscious: Self-Observation, Self-Reflection, Self-Revelation, Self-Honesty, and Self-Awareness*

Through honest self-observation, I recognize that what I experience, judge, understand, and/or perceive about my experiences and life, I am interpreting through the filters of my belief system and perceptions.

These two – beliefs and perceptions – create the version of reality I am living. To shift my interpretations, I choose to "hold" the following awareness':

- *"No one and nothing is against me."*[69]
- My perceptions are just that, my perceptions, and they have nothing to do with others, or what they are experiencing.
- Conscious choices create new realities and ways to see things differently.
- "It's not about me!" [70] It may feel like it is, but it isn't.
- The ego takes everything personally and feels diminished.
- "Life has only the meaning I give it!"
- *"What am I making this experience mean?"*[71]
- *"I have experience, experiences do not have me."*

The infinite –Q- field of possibility (wave) collapses in order to create form (particle) – this is just a reminder that I am always free to choose again.

---

[68] **Nemeth, Maria, Ph.D. (MCC, Master Certified Coach). Academy for Coaching Excellence. Sacramento, CA.**
[69] Simmons, Gary. *I of the Storm*. Unity House. Unity Village, MO. 2001
[70] Nemeth, Maria, Ph.D. (MCC, Master Certified Coach). Academy for Coaching Excellence. Sacramento, CA.
[71] Simmons, Gary. *I of the Storm*. Unity House. Unity Village, MO. 2001

4. BE Aligned with the Field of Infinite Possibilities: Take a -Q- Presence Pause

I consciously choose to participate in self-observation and self-honesty; they are the cornerstones of awakening. I consciously engage the acts of self-observation and self- honesty as I turn my attention interiorly by taking frequent Presence Pauses. When taking a Presence Pause I consciously:

Pause
  (I pause and breathe, align w/ field, and *BE* conscious and present
      to the energies arising within and around me.)
Observe
  (I notice and be interested in what is arising energetically in the
  field and in the moment and in what I am thinking, feeling and/or
  sensing about what is happening.)
Align
  (After I notice, I tell the truth, first, to myself about what I am
  thinking, feeling, and/or sensing as I align with the energies
  presenting themselves.)
Act
  (I take authentic action as guided by the –Q– field, my *inner*
  witness, intuition, and/or synchro-divinity).

5. BE Impeccable: The –Q– Shift – Shifting Awareness

How fast I can shift my awareness in the midst of a chaotic experience or a situation determines how awake or energetically conscious I am in the moment. I shift my awareness in situations through asking and/or choosing the following:

- "What am I making this experience mean?"
- "Am I willing to be changed by what I see?"[72]
- "Am I willing to shift my attention from "being right to doing right" and "seeing life and its experiences through a different lens" (a different viewing point)?
- "Am I willing to shift my attention from "being right to doing
- right," in this situation?"
- No judgment, just interest, as in an unbiased observation.
- I am responsible for my life according to the choices I make, thus I choose to make conscious choices.

[72] Simmons, Gary. *I of the Storm.* Unity House. Unity Village, MO. 2001

- I know that dying is a part of living, thus, I willingly surrender and "die" to old aspects of self/ego that are no longer serving my highest and best good.
- I change at depth, as I consciously participate in self-honesty, self-observation, living authentically, and choosing to *BE*.
- I choose to face my deepest fears and receiving the gift of learning – who I am.
- "What do I notice and does what I notice interest me?"

6.   *BE Accountable: Use Conscious Skilled Behaviors*

"*Conflict is a sign that my soul is ready to grow*"[73], therefore, I choose to use conscious, skilled behaviors to enhance my life experiences. I am aware that conflict arises out of the use of unskilled behaviors. When I live unskillfully, I create suffering and pain, which arises out of being out of alignment with the energies of the present moment. Unskilled behaviors occur when I am unconscious, reactive, and/or confused. To "sin" means to miss the "high mark" of human existence by using unskilled behaviors. Skilled behaviors and key elements that can shift from a space of conflict to a consciousness of peace are and occur when:

- I release the need to be right and make "doing the right thing" more interesting than being right.
- I realize that: "What I resist persists."
- I explore the common ground that exists among & between us.
- I do not take things personally; things happen that may or may not have anything to do with me.
- What I do about what happens is what is important – will I choose to express love or fear – and how quickly can I shift my awareness around what is happening.
- I trust the process
- I see value in multiple (and others) perspectives
- I know everyone has a need to be loved
- I am willing to make amends
- I say "Thank you!"
- I see everyone as whole – not broken or needing to be fixed
- I get out of victim mentality
- I hold the vision for a greater possibility to occur

[73] Simmons, Gary. *I of the Storm*. Unity House. Unity Village, MO. 2001

7. *BE*!

*I shift my awareness to be interested in wholeness and to *BE*
  wholeness in action. To *BE* wholeness in action I consciously
  know that:
*It is not about what I do, but who I *BE* as I do it!
*My work is to *BE*, to *BE* conscious of the –Q- energy field as it
  arises in each moment and what it is revealing – to notice and be
  interested.
*I *BE* the state of awareness, the state of consciousness, I want to see;
  instead of desiring or wishing, that it (peace, love, joy, etc.) was
  here or that someone else was showing up as it.

- *BE* non-attached, non-resistant, and non-judgment (J.A.R.)
- *BE* self-aware and self-observant
- *BE* generous of spirit, time, talent, and money
- *BE* self-less service
- *BE* change in expression and action, *BE* authentic action
- *BE* integrity, *BE* honest, *BE* the flow, *BE* vision
- *BE* present, *BE* attentive, *BE* aligned energetically w/-Q-
- *BE* respect, for self and others. BE the meditative flow.
- *BE* open and A.L.L.O.W. - *Always Let Light Open the Way*
- *BE* prayer in action and *BE* contemplative and *BE* prayed up
- *BE* the non-anxious presence in the room
- *BE* energetically spacious in heart and mind

*I shift my awareness, from what seems to be "missing, broken, or not
working" in the situation, other persons, or myself, to being more
interested in "Who I came here to *BE*" and how I am living and
expressing my (core) values or not.

*I *BE* conscious and aware of energy as it reveals itself as intuition,
intuitive hits and/or synchronistic (synchro-divinity) experiences. I *BE*
the meditative flow.

*I *BE* conscious as I *BE* more interested in what is arising
energetically in the – Q- field - as a lesson or learning – than in what
appears to be happening, as the drama of the moment.

The End or Just the Beginning?

Humankind is on the verge of a quantum transformation in consciousness; the evolutionary pulse is beating a new drum and creating a new rhythm for change. This change of mind and heart has the potential for tremendous impact on the way we handle our personal and professional affairs.

From the various leadership and life models that we have perused throughout this book, we can conclude that as human conditions shift values shift. As values, shift the next level of growth for the human condition follow. It is all a natural part of the spiraling circle of evolution.

In order to remain in the flow of what is happening throughout the spiral of evolution, humankind will have to adapt or possibly, die out. This is not about doom and gloom. This is about humankind honestly "seeing" what is in front of them – energetically – as a collective whole.

The time for conscious choice is drawing near. We cannot continue to pollute our waters, send nuclear materials into the heart of mother earth, use our reserves as if there is no tomorrow to consider, and so on and so on and think that it will not at some point come back to haunt us.

Throughout this book, we have reviewed many venues and teachings around personal growth, observing self, generous listening, awakening, -Q-transformation, and generally, gaining new awareness' for life and living. We have reviewed practical tools, exercises, models, theories, etc., and collectively these have provided the reader with an opportunity to either look at hidden patterns of behaviors and/or to review and assess current values and levels of conscious awareness.

Humankind now has the capacity to understand how to work consciously with the energies that surround them and to use this energy for the creation of goals and intentions that support the highest and best for all involved – within the range of our individual stage of growth and associated decision-making capabilities.

Through conscious engagement with the ideas presented in this book, each of us can envision and initiate new courses of authentic action for our lives. Never think that your opinion or your actions do not count.

As each of us makes the decision to, and participates in conscious authentic actions, and does this on both a personal level and professional level – we have the capacity to lead humankind into a new future and into new ways of doing and *BE*-ing in the world. Go forth and fearlessly add your ideas and your voice to the world!

Glossary

"A-holic": a suffix that connotes a negative behavior is associated with the word to which it is connected. "A-holic" behaviors do not fulfill anything; they are a result of being in the void of forgetfulness.

Authentic-Self Actions (internal choices) *and Authentic Actions* (external movement): both are a result of a combination of conscious awareness, self-observation, self-honesty, and conscious choice/s. All of which combine and allow for an outcome that holds for the highest and best for all persons involved and that is specific, attainable, measurable, relative, and time-based (external).

BE: 1- BE a state of awareness – we consciously *BE* Peace, *BE* Love, *BE* Authentic, etc. we no longer seek these things, we *BE* them). An active state of consciously <u>BE-</u>ing in tune with the energy field that arises around us.

Conscious: to BE conscious means that we stop and take notice and we are interested in what we are noticing. We are conscious we have the capacity to honestly, look at what is happening around and within us, energetically, and make changes. By being conscious we are open to the possibility of participating in our experiences in a more cognizant manner.

Dancing at the Edge of Mystery (DEM): is a metaphor and a symbol for those moments in life when our soul and the "Universe" (invisible, universal unified-energy field) invites us to participate at new levels and awareness' in consciousness. The invitation is to create more conscious choices, participate in awakening through self-observation, self-questioning, self-reflection, prayer, contemplation, meditation, and/or the taking of authentic-self actions. DEM is where seeking stops and a consciousness of *BE* is initiated.

God: <u>S</u>elf, <u>E</u>ssence, the Energy underpinning the Universe, Unchanging, Eternal, all-powerful. Known by different names according to the beliefs of the spiritual tradition. Adverse ego-self has forgotten its divinity and acts as such.

Integral: refers to that which is vital, primary, embracing, balancing, inclusive, essential, and central. When referred to in the context of human beings integral means, *"models, maps, and practices that include the full spectrum of human potentials"*. We develop an integral perspective physical, mentally, emotionally, and spiritually as we successfully integrate the various states and stages of development; e.g., Maslow's Hierarchy of Needs

Intuition: *"...natural knowing capacity, inner knowing; ... wisdom of the heart, immediate apprehension of ...Truth without resort to intellectual means... "*

Principle: the primary source of something, an important underlying law or assumption required in a system of thought. Unchanging, eternal, forever true.

Quantum Physics: a knowledge that supports and reveals an understanding of the life at the energetic, quantum level; the level of the smallest discrete quantity of a physical property. Quantum research measures not only the smallest unit of a physical property, but also what happens with its energy as the quanta unit moves about.

Spirit: the vital force that characterizes a human being as being alive. Enthusiasm and energy, a state of mind.

Synchronicity: random appearing events, that your soul attracts into your life to help you evolve or to place emphasis on something going on in your life.

Truth: Unbounded unity.

"Void of Forgetfulness": when we go in search of that ubiquitous something, thinking it "lives" outside of ourselves, in someone else or something else in this material world. We are living without an understanding of the essence of the holy or whole person that we *BE*.

Unconscious: the opposite of conscious, we are "asleep" and do not take notice and/or are not interested in what is occurring around us, energetically.

Unified (energetic) Field (-Q-): energy coming together to form a single unit or entity, such as in a thought-field or morphic field. This invisible, infinite, energetic, resonant, quantum-unified field is referred to in this book as -Q-.

The Power of BE! – Seven Week Study Guide

Basic Weekly Format:
>   1. Opening prayer
>   2. Group discussion of practices and concepts of chapter
>   3. Q& A about topic
>   4 Weekly Reflective Question (WRQ):
>   *"What did you learn about yourself (this week) as a result of having consciously engaged with the material in this chapter?"*

Week 1: Introduction and Chapter 1
1.   What does it mean in your life, to *"Dance at the Edge of Mystery?"*
2.   What is the *Void of Forgetfulness*?
3.   What is the *–Q- field* and what meaning does it have for our lives?
4.   WRQ

Week 2: Chapter Two
1.   What does engaging with *"YES"* mean for your life?
2.   Are you ready to speak your *"YES"* into the substance, the evolutionary pulse of the universe and what does that mean?
3.   WRQ

Week 3: Chapter Three
1.   What does– *Shadow Dancing* – really mean for our lives?
2.   How did we form the egoic self?
3.   WRQ

Week 4: Chapter Four
1.   What is the relationship between quantum concepts and spiritual principles, and their correlation to *Conscious -Q- Creation*?
2.   What is a responsible, conscious choice?
3.   WRQ

Week 5: Chapter Five
1.   What is the difference between Newtonian Perspectives and Quantum "living" Systems?
2.   What meaning, if any, does the –Q- perspective have for your life?
3.   WRQ

Week 6: Chapter Five (Continued)
1.   What impact of Quantum Principles on leadership and management styles?
2.   How do Quantum leadership styles differ from Newtonian styles?
3.   In what instances would one be used over the other?
4.   WRQ

Week 7: Chapter Six
1.   What is a BE! Building Block? What value to they hold for our lives and for creating a living reality of a prepared consciousness?
2.   What does it mean to live as *BE*?
3.   What have you personally learned about yourself because of having consciously engaged with this book and its curriculum? **WRQ**

About The Author

Toni G. Boehm, M.S.N., Ph.D.
Revtboehm@aol.com   www.toniboehm.com   816-304-3044(c)

Toni G. Boehm is an inspirational and dynamic speaker, author, minister, poet, nurse practitioner and known for her passionate teaching style and her expertise in the facilitation of classes on spiritual growth, transformation, and mysticism.

For over twenty years Boehm served at the world headquarters of Unity School of Christianity, Unity Village, MO. She currently serves as adjunct faculty at Unity, is a certified Peace-maker and Transition Consultant, certified Spiral Intelligence Coach, and a spiritual life and organization coach, a leadership and curriculum consultant, a workshop and retreat facilitator. As a consultant, Boehm reviews and develops the best standards of practices for spiritual communities, and provides leadership teams with board training and assistance in developing vision, mission, core values, and strategic-long range plans.

During her career at Unity, she held the positions of Dean of Administration/Unity School of Religious Studies; Director/ Strategic Initiatives; Vice President/Education, and as a member of Unity's Executive Team. Teaching internationally Boehm facilitates classes and seminars on prayer, prosperity, spiritual and personal empowerment, transformation, awakening the feminine nature of the divine, spiritual leadership skill development, and Quantum Transformation. Through her work, Boehm assists others in personal and transformation awakenings.

Boehm introduces students to the spiritual knowledge and skills necessary for living their lives from their highest innate potential. Her personal mission statement is:

"I am a midwife for the birthing of the soul's remembrance".

Boehm has held positions at the world headquarters of Hallmark Cards, Inc. and the American Nurses Association.
She is past recipient of University of Missouri's, Woman's Council Award for Research and her master's research thesis was presented at John's Hopkins Medical Symposium. She is listed in Marquis' Who's Who in American Women and Who's Who in America. Boehm is author of numerous articles and the books including:
*The Spiritual Intrapreneur
*One Day My Mouth Just Opened
*Embracing the Feminine Nature of the Divine
*Luminous Darkness:
*The Power of YES!
*Conscious "Living"

To schedule a board retreat, workshop, etc. or to purchase her books and CD's call 816-304-3044 or e-mail revtboehm@aol.com

CPSIA information can be obtained at www.ICGtesting.com
Printed in the USA
LVOW090521291011

252504LV00002B/8/P